Cocktails

Southern Style

Cocktails
Southern Style

POURS, DRINKS, SIPS, AND BITES

BELINDA SMITH-SULLIVAN

Photographs by Lauren McDuffie

Gibbs Smith

To Bonnie, Barbara, Betty, and Lottie . . .
friends forever! And to Monique, who will keep
the tradition going!

First Edition
29 28 27 26 25   5 4 3 2 1

Published by
Gibbs Smith
570 N. Sportsplex Dr.
Kaysville, Utah 84037
1.800.835.4993 orders
www.gibbs-smith.com

Designed by Sheryl Dickert
Production design by Renee Bond
Printed and bound in China

This product is made of FSC®-certified and other controlled
material.

Library of Congress Control Number: 2024942289
ISBN: 978-1-4236-6605-9
Ebook ISBN: 978-1-4236-6606-6

Contents

Foreword 6

Introduction 9

Anatomy of the Cocktail 9

The Golden Rules of Bartending 11

Cocktail-Making Equipment 12

Basic Cocktail-Making Techniques 13

SIMPLE SYRUPS AND INFUSED VODKAS 15

CELEBRATE 20

RISE AND SHINE 35

PORCH SIPPIN' 50

ULTIMATE SOUTHERN-INSPIRED MARTINIS 64

FIVE O'CLOCK SOMEWHERE 75

SPRITZES, SMASHES, AND FARTS 84

SHANDIES AND BEER COCKTAILS 92

ALMOST COCKTAILS 103

CLASSIC SOUTHERN COCKTAILS 112

NIBBLES AND BITES 124

Acknowledgments 140

Index 141

About the Author 144

Foreword

As a child, visiting my grandfather, I learned many things. Not least among these was that the time between five and six p.m. was devoted to something called "cocktail hour," a sacrosanct assembly of the adults in the living room with its view of the Georgia hills. My grandfather was hardly a mixologist—as I recall the options were Scotch and soda, Scotch and water, or Scotch on the rocks—but he would pour the drinks and the adults would gather around a coffee table bearing a bowl of peanuts and some cheese and crackers. Whatever cares had plagued them during the day disappeared as they spent an hour in conversation, sipping their drinks and watching the golden afternoon sun move across the rolling meadows. If I made an appearance, I would be rewarded with a smear of cheese ball on a Ritz cracker and maybe even my grandfather's own twist on a Shirley Temple (he made it with Sprite instead of ginger ale and we called it a "Grandpa Candler"). Life was good and cocktail hour, I learned from even my modest participation, was a time for camaraderie and relaxation—a time that seemed to exist outside the ordinary progression of the clock.

From those childhood days, I learned the importance of pausing, taking a little time each day to value friends and family and forget about work and worry. In adulthood, I have learned something else about cocktail hour: it offers endless opportunities for creativity. It turns out there are liquors other than Scotch and mixers other than water and soda. My cocktail cabinet now has bourbon and bitters; my refrigerator has a jar of cherries and a bottle of simple syrup; and oranges and limes are always on the counter in case I'm in need of a twist. During COVID I took the opportunity to explore mixology, adapting recipes to my own peculiar taste (my Maple Old Fashioned is a house favorite).

The cheese and crackers and roasted peanuts of my youth have been replaced with something called *charcuterie*, which even my eight-year-old self would have seen as a big improvement. Cocktail hour now can be a meal, a time that extends past six o'clock and is celebrated with a board heaped with meats and cheeses and craft beverages that would have been unrecognizable to my grandfather. And what boundless opportunities for our creative impulses those charcuterie boards and cocktails provide.

But at its heart, cocktail hour remains unchanged. Whether sipping Scotch neat or imbibing a cocktail that leaves the counter scattered with bottles, implements, and the detritus of various fruits, cocktail hour is about relationships. It's about calling a time-out on the cares of the day and raising a glass with people you love. I've been lucky enough to raise a glass with Belinda Smith-Sullivan and share that golden hour with her. I hope, through the recipes in this book, you'll find the time to do the same with your family and friends. And if, by chance, you find yourself clinking glasses with the people who bring joy to your life at some other time of day, as my grandfather would say, "It's five o'clock somewhere!"

Charlie Lovett
***New York Times* bestselling author**
The Bookman's Tale
The Enigma Affair
Lewis Carroll: Formed by Faith

Introduction

I like bars! There is just something about bars that bring out all my curiosity. When I am at a restaurant, I like to belly up to the bar instead of sitting off to the side or in the formal dining room. I am constantly asking the bartenders questions as they are mixing cocktails: Why are you doing this or that and what purpose does it serve? How does it enhance the cocktail experience? And if you had to substitute something, how or what would that look like? Perhaps I missed my calling. . . . Cocktails fascinate me! In culinary school, my two favorite courses were bartending and wine hospitality. So much so that I have single-handedly amassed a collection of liquors, liqueurs, wines, bitters, and, yes, even craft beers, that would rival the best of bars. Oh, for experimental purposes, of course . . .

A true art form, bartending deserves a lot more credit than it receives. If you have ever been to an exceptional bar and witnessed the true talent of bartenders, you know what I'm talking about. Not even Tom Cruise understands the depth of this true talent.

It is hard to imagine any occasion, special or otherwise, when a cocktail is *not* appropriate, expected, or just plain wanted! When you think of all the ways we celebrate—weddings, funerals, birthdays, new births, promotions, retirements, homecomings, holidays—wherever a toast is warranted, there is a cocktail involved.

No one knows this better than Southerners! We live our lives celebrating something . . . all the time. I would like to believe that the first cocktail party ever happened in the South! Maybe that's where the concept of hospitality got its start.

So, let's slow down and channel the Southern hospitality that exists in all of us. Celebrate *something* today and invite new friends or old friends or both to enjoy one of your favorite cocktails. CHEERS!

ANATOMY OF THE COCKTAIL

As with cooking or creating a recipe, the same principle of establishing a flavor profile holds true for developing and building a cocktail. Once you understand these basics you are on your way to becoming a home bartender.

A cocktail consists of these elements:

MAIN ALCOHOL

This is the base alcohol of a cocktail—such as bourbon, tequila, vodka, or gin—and is often, although not always, where the cocktail derives its name. It will always be the major alcoholic component in a drink.

SECONDARY ALCOHOL

This is the accent alcohol added for extra flavor and to complement the base alcohol.

SWEETENING AGENT

This is juice or syrup added to the cocktail, and is used to complement and bring out the flavors of the alcohol while also acting as a binder.

BITTERS

These are cocktail seasonings, like herbs and spices, derived from barks, flowers, roots, and citrus peels, to name a few. They offset the acidity of the other flavor profiles of a cocktail to create a smoother drink. They are used in small parts or dashes.

GARNISH

This is the artistic component of a cocktail, like a lemon or lime twist, an orange peel, or a lemon wedge. It can even be herbs such as lavender, basil, and rosemary, depending on the flavor profile of the drink. This gives your cocktail the wow factor.

Strategies for creating your own signature cocktails

INFUSION

Infusing vodkas and simple syrups with herbs, fruits, vegetables, peppers, and spices can offer a unique spin on traditional cocktails.

THE SWAP

Take a recipe you already know, like a screwdriver. Replace the orange juice with grapefruit juice and you have a Greyhound. Or swap out the white wine for a kir and substitute with champagne and now you have a kir royale.

THE 2:1:1 FORMULA/RATIO

This formula represents the ratio of ingredients that should yield a perfect drink. Translated, it means 2 parts alcohol to 1 part of something sweet and 1 part of something sour. So, if you do not have a recipe and would like to try something for the first time, use this ratio to start. You can always adjust to your liking.

THE GOLDEN RULES OF BARTENDING

Start with the classics

If you have a favorite cocktail, research the original recipe to discover how it was developed. Then, and only then, can you experiment with or alter it.

Alcohol is the most important ingredient

The alcohol content of a cocktail should be 50 percent. Even if you prefer a "lighter" version of a cocktail, when making a cocktail for someone else use the proper ratio.

Ice is the second most important ingredient

Do not skimp on the ice. Have plenty on hand when throwing a cocktail party. You will need it for blending and for filling the glasses.

Keep it simple

You will not need to stock your bar with every liquor or liqueur on the market. Have your favorites on hand and learn how to make variations of the same recipes. See notes on swapping on page 10.

A cocktail should have balance

What you are aiming for is a drink that is not too sweet, too bitter, or too boozy! The last sip should taste as good as the first.

A cocktail should have visual appeal

As in eating, we drink first with our eyes. Presentation is everything, so pay attention to garnishing drinks and icing glasses when necessary.

Mixers

The other additives that you may include in your cocktails are called mixers, known as club soda, tonic water, sparkling mineral water, or various soft drinks. Be very particular about the mixers used in your cocktails. Read the labels carefully. Use mixers that contain as many fresh or natural ingredients as possible.

Only shake cocktails that have juice in them

Cocktails are either aromatic, meaning they contain only alcoholic ingredients, or they are sours, which contain citrus fruit juices. Sours require shaking, which slightly dilutes the tanginess of the fruit introduced. Martinis are never shaken, only stirred! Enough said about that.

COCKTAIL-MAKING EQUIPMENT

If you would like to explore the wonderful world of cocktails, and you were thinking of planning, organizing, and equipping a bar cart in the comfort of your home, there are just a few basic pieces of equipment you will need . . . in addition to all the bottles of liquor!

Channel Knife

Used to peel fruit rinds into thin strips, like those used in martinis.

Citrus Juicer

A handheld juicer used to squeeze citrus and extract juice.

Fine-Mesh Strainer

Used for double-straining drinks and removing any seeds, stems, ice, or other solids that may remain as the result of muddling.

Jigger

A measuring tool, usually two-sided, used for measuring and pouring liquor into the mixing glass or shaker. A jigger prevents you from over- or under-pouring. Standard jiggers come with two conjoining cups, one larger than the other.

Mixing Glass

There is a type of mixing glass specifically designed for stirring ingredients. It can also be used with or without the need of a strainer.

Muddler

A tool designed to smash and mix herbs and fruit added to cocktails and strained out of the cocktail once it is shaken.

Shaker/Mixing Glass

A metal container used to mix alcoholic beverages. The most common shaker comes in two parts, the metal bottom and the glass mixing container. They are inserted into each other for shaking or used separately for stirring or muddling. This shaker requires a separate strainer.

Spoon

A long slender spoon for stirring cocktails. Use with the above-mentioned mixing glass.

Strainer

A cocktail strainer is used to remove ice from a drink once it has been made and is being poured. The small holes in the strainer allow only liquid to pass through.

Y-Shaped Peeler

Used to make very thin pieces of citrus peel for cocktails.

BASIC COCKTAIL-MAKING TECHNIQUES

Here are some fundamental cocktail-making techniques every bartender needs to know.

Layering

The purpose of layering is to create district layers in a drink. It involves pouring lighter, less-dense liquids on top of heavier ones. The less alcohol means the more sugar there is, therefore the heavier the ingredient will be. The heavier ingredients should be poured first.

Hold the spoon with the back facing upward, pressing lightly against the inside of the glass to steady it. Slowly and steadily, pour the ingredient over the back of the spoon so that it gently settles without disturbing the layer below it.

This requires practice, so it may take time to get it right. However, this does not mean the drink is bad; pour it into another glass over ice and enjoy.

Muddling

In muddling, the purpose is to extract the essential oils from herb or fruit in the drink. This can be accomplished with a muddler or a wooden spoon.

Using a glass or a cocktail shaker, place the ingredients in the bottom and gently press down on them while twisting the muddler at the same time. Repeating this motion about five times should be sufficient.

Shaking

A cocktail is shaken to mix the ingredients thoroughly while adding dilution. In cocktails that contain egg whites, the shaking whips the eggs into a foam.

Make sure the lid of the shaker is in place. Hold the shaker firmly and, pointing it away from yourself and others, shake vigorously over your shoulders for 10 to 15 seconds.

Stirring

The purpose of stirring a cocktail is to gently dilute it with the ice to make it more palatable.

Place the bar spoon inside the glass, and while holding the spoon at the top, gently rotate the spoon around the inside of the glass for 10 to 15 rotations.

SIMPLE SYRUPS AND
INFUSED VODKAS

> "Cocktails: the ultimate alchemy
> of flavors and spirits."
> —Unknown

By making these infused vodkas and syrups, you will be able to create and mix your own craft cocktails. Make as much as you like—infused vodkas will last forever unless you drink it all! Package some in pretty containers and give as gifts to friends and family.

Do experiment with other herbs, spices, and flavors of your liking and try combining your favorite flavors. There are endless possibilities.

SIMPLE SYRUPS

A liquid sweetener to use in any hot or cold beverage that calls for the addition of granulated sugar, simple syrups dissolve quicker and totally and do not leave behind a gritty taste or feel. Use simple syrups in cocktails, coffee, and tea. They are also ideal for drizzling on ice cream or cake for additional moistness.

Plain Simple Syrup

MAKES 2 CUPS

2 cups sugar
2 cups water

Combine the sugar and water in a medium saucepan over medium heat. Bring to a boil and stir until sugar dissolves. Remove from the heat and allow to steep for 15 minutes. Strain with a mesh strainer into a sterilized jar. Let cool, tighten lid, label, and store in the refrigerator.

Rosemary Simple Syrup

MAKES 2 CUPS

2 cups sugar
2 cups water
½ cup rosemary leaves

Combine the sugar, water, and rosemary in a medium saucepan over medium heat. Bring to a boil and stir until sugar dissolves. Remove from the heat and allow to steep for 15 minutes. Strain with a mesh strainer into a sterilized jar. Let cool, tighten lid, label, and store in the refrigerator.

Mint Simple Syrup

2 cups sugar

2 cups water

½ cup fresh mint leaves

Combine the sugar, water, and mint in a medium saucepan over medium heat. Bring to a boil and stir until sugar dissolves. Remove from the heat and allow to steep for 15 minutes. Strain with a mesh strainer into a sterilized jar. Let cool, tighten lid, label, and store in the refrigerator.

Lavender Simple Syrup

2 cups sugar

2 cups water

2 tablespoons fresh lavender flowers

Combine the sugar, water, and lavender in a medium saucepan over medium heat. Bring to a boil and stir until sugar dissolves. Remove from the heat and allow to steep for 15 minutes. Strain with a mesh strainer into a sterilized jar. Let cool, tighten lid, label, and store in the refrigerator.

Spiced-Honey Syrup

MAKES 1 CUP

½ cup water
½ cup honey
2 fresh rosemary sprigs
2 cinnamon sticks
1 tablespoon cardamon pods or ½ teaspoon ground cardamom
1-inch piece fresh ginger, sliced
Zest of an orange
1 teaspoon vanilla extract

Combine the water, honey, rosemary, cinnamon, cardamom, and ginger in a medium saucepan. Bring to a boil over high heat and boil for 3 minutes. Remove from the heat and stir in the orange zest and vanilla. Strain into a sterilized jar. Let cool, tighten lid, label, and store in the refrigerator.

ROSEMARY-INFUSED VODKA

MAKES 750 MILLILITERS

3 rosemary sprigs
1 bottle (750 milliliters) premium vodka

Rinse the rosemary and pat dry. Place it into a quart mason jar or other jar of choice with a tight-fitting lid. Pour the vodka into the jar and seal tightly. Shake and then store in a cool, dry place for 3 to 5 days. On the third day test the vodka, and when at your desired taste strain the rosemary, using a fine strainer lined with clean cheesecloth. Label and store the same as you would other vodka products.

CHILI-INFUSED VODKA

MAKES 750 MILLILITERS

3 red chiles
1 bottle (750 milliliters) premium vodka

Rinse the chiles, slice in half, and remove the seeds. Place the chiles into a quart mason jar or other jar of choice with a tight-fitting lid. Pour the vodka into the jar and seal tightly. Shake and then store in a cool, dry place for 1 to 3 days. On the second day test the vodka, and when at your desired taste strain the chiles, using a fine strainer lined with clean cheesecloth. Label and store the same as you would other vodka products.

CARDAMOM, CINNAMON, AND STAR ANISE–INFUSED VODKA

MAKES 750 MILLILITERS

10 cardamom pods
3 cinnamon sticks
10 star anise pods
1 bottle (750 milliliters) premium vodka

Place the cardamom, cinnamon, and star anise into a quart mason jar or other jar of choice with a tight-fitting lid. Pour the vodka into the jar and seal tightly. Shake and then store in a cool, dry place for 5 to 7 days. On the fifth day test the vodka, and when at your desired taste strain the spices, using a fine strainer lined with clean cheesecloth. Label and store the same as you would other vodka products.

CELEBRATE

"Cocktails are a celebration
of the fine balance between
taste and presentation."
—Unknown

The months of November and December include two of
our largest holidays of the year and bring us ultimate
celebration opportunities. The cocktails that accompany
these festivities are special and can be elaborate. Take
advantage of this joyful, family-oriented time together
to showcase some of these cocktails that are designed to
put you in the spirit of celebrating.

SOIXANTE-QUINZE (FRENCH 75)

The French 75 cocktail, although originating at Harry's Bar in New York, was popularized by Arnaud's French 75 Bar in New Orleans. Arnaud's, a fourth-generation restaurant, is considered the grande dame of creole cuisine and has been recognized by the James Beard Foundation for its Outstanding Bar Program.

SERVES 1

1 ½ ounces cognac
1 teaspoon freshly squeezed lemon juice
¼ teaspoon Plain Simple Syrup (page 16)
2 ¾ ounces champagne or sparkling wine
Lemon twist, for garnish

GLASS: champagne tulip or flute

In a shaker filled with ice, combine the cognac, lemon juice, and simple syrup. Shake until chilled. Strain into the glass and top with champagne and add the lemon twist.

MISSISSIPPI EGGNOG

Eggnog is one of those Christmas holiday beverages that has been a tradition in our house since . . . well, forever. My parents are from Mississippi, so naturally I thought it was just a punch—of sorts—from the Delta. I never knew it had alcohol in it, as my parents were not drinkers, but it always seemed to make everyone happy when it was served.

SERVES 8

8 large egg yolks
¾ cup sugar
1 cup heavy cream
2 cups milk
½ teaspoon cinnamon, plus more for serving
½ teaspoon nutmeg, plus more for serving
1 vanilla bean, split, and seeds scraped
¼ to ½ cup bourbon or rum
Whipped cream (optional)

GLASS: punch glasses or cups

In a large bowl using a hand mixer, beat the egg yolks and sugar together until light in color. In a medium saucepan over medium heat, combine the cream, milk, cinnamon, and nutmeg. Heat, stirring often, until the mixture reaches a simmer. Add the hot milk to the egg mixture, a little at a time to temper, whisking constantly. When all the hot milk has been added, pour the entire mixture back into the saucepan. Whisk constantly until the mixture thickens and coats the back of a wooden spoon or until it reaches 160 degrees F on an instant-read thermometer.

Remove from the heat and add the vanilla seeds and alcohol. Strain the mixture through a mesh strainer into a large bowl or pitcher. Cover and refrigerate. Chill for at least 1 hour. Serve with whipped cream (if using), and sprinkle with additional cinnamon or nutmeg.

MERRY CRANBERRY MIMOSA

A mimosa cocktail most often consists of orange juice and champagne, but there is a lot of room for creativity with all the juices and combinations that are available: pineapple, pomegranate, grapefruit, raspberry, and more. Add to that a splash of a similar flavored liqueur for an extra boost, and you have a truly exceptional mimosa experience.

SERVES 1

Cranberry juice
½ ounce orange liqueur (triple sec, Cointreau, or Grand Marnier)
Champagne or sparkling wine
Fresh cranberries, for garnish
Rosemary sprig, for garnish
Orange twist, for garnish

GLASS: champagne flute

Fill the champagne flute ⅓ full with cranberry juice. Add the orange liqueur and top off with champagne. Garnish with fresh cranberries, rosemary, and orange twist.

BOURBON AND HONEY-SPICE COCKTAIL

This cocktail elevates the traditional old-fashioned with the flavors of honey and warming spices.

SERVES 1

2 ounces bourbon
1 ounce freshly squeezed lemon juice
1 ounce freshly squeezed orange juice
1 to 2 dashes orange bitters
1 to 2 ounces Spiced-Honey Syrup (page 18)
Rosemary sprig, for garnish
Orange and lemon wheels, for garnish
Cinnamon sticks (optional)

GLASS: rocks

In a shaker, combine the bourbon, lemon juice, orange juice, and bitters and 2 to 3 tablespoons Spiced-Honey Syrup. Add ice and shake until chilled. Strain into the glass and garnish as desired.

HOT BUTTERED RUM

This favorite winter drink is irresistible no matter what part of the country you live in. A true Southerner knows this as a hot toddy, *with whiskey substituted for the rum. No matter where you're from or whatever your preference of whiskey or rum, you are probably not going to find a cocktail that will warm you up faster!*

SERVES 1

2 teaspoons packed light brown sugar
1 tablespoon unsalted butter, softened
Splash vanilla extract
1 dash ground cinnamon
1 dash allspice
1 dash nutmeg
2 ounces dark rum
4 ounces hot water
Cinnamon stick, for garnish

GLASS: Irish coffee

Place the sugar, butter, vanilla, cinnamon, allspice, and nutmeg into the bottom of the glass and mix well. Pour in the rum and top with hot water. Stir well and garnish with the cinnamon stick.

IRISH COFFEE

The ultimate after-dinner cocktail, Irish coffee is easy to make at home. If your dinner menu ends with a chocolate course, Irish coffee is the perfect accompaniment, as the bitterness of the chocolate enhances the flavors of the coffee and whiskey. You can't go wrong here! I brought this recipe home from the Old Town Whiskey Bar at Bodega in Cork.

SERVES 1

Unsweetened heavy cream, for garnish
1 teaspoon brown sugar
1 shot Jameson Irish Whiskey
4 to 6 ounces hot coffee

GLASS: Irish coffee

Lightly whip the cream. It should not form peaks but should be thick enough to float. Set aside.

Fill the glass with hot water and let it set for several minutes, then discard the water. Add the sugar and whiskey to the heated glass. Fill with coffee, leaving a 1- to 2-finger space at the top of glass, and give one full stir. When coffee stops swirling, slowly float the cream off the back of a spoon, up to the rim of the glass.

MULLED WINE

Simmering your favorite red wine with a variety of warming spices and brandy transform the ordinary into the extraordinary. Cabernet sauvignon, merlot, and Malbecs are the ideal choices here, but choose whatever red wine you like to drink.

SERVES 6

1 bottle red wine
1 orange, sliced, plus more for garnish
6 whole cloves
3 cinnamon sticks, plus more for garnish
3 star anise pods, plus more for garnish
¼ cup honey
½ cup brandy

GLASS: Irish coffee

Combine all the ingredients in a medium saucepan over medium heat. Bring to a simmer—do not allow to boil. Simmer for 10 minutes. Ladle into glasses and garnish with an orange slice, cinnamon stick, and star anise.

Cider Sidecar

CIDER SIDECAR

This recipe takes the traditional sidecar combination of cognac, Cointreau, and lemon and adds one of the South's favorite nonalcoholic beverages to the mix. Apple cider just turned into a grown-up treat.

SERVES 1

2 ounces fresh apple cider
2 ounces cognac
1 ounce Cointreau
1 ounce freshly squeezed lemon juice
Lemon twists, for rimming and garnish
Granulated sugar, for rimming
Apple wheels (optional)

GLASS: champagne coupe

Pour the cider, cognac, Cointreau, and lemon juice into a shaker, and top with ice. Shake until very chilled. Rub the rim of the glass with a piece of lemon zest, then dip the rim of the glass into the sugar. Strain the cocktail into the coupe and garnish with lemon twist and apple wheels (if using).

CHAMPAGNE COCKTAIL

If no holiday celebration is complete without champagne, then champagne is the quintessential guest of honor!

SERVES 1

1 sugar cube
3 to 5 dashes Angostura bitters
Champagne or sparkling wine, chilled
Lemon twist, for garnish
Natural maraschino cherry (optional)

GLASS: chilled champagne flute

Drop the sugar cube into the chilled champagne flute and douse with 3 to 5 dashes of Angostura bitters. Fill the glass with champagne, garnish with the lemon twist, and drop the cherry (if using) into the bottom of the glass.

NEW ORLEANS CITRUS-POMEGRANATE PUNCH

Anyone who has ever been to New Orleans knows that just being there is one big party. So leave it to residents of that city to know how to supersize a good drink when it's needed. This punch will serve a crowd and leave you with more time to enjoy your guests.

SERVES 12

¼ cup granulated sugar

1 cup pomegranate juice

2 bottles (750 milliliters each) champagne or sparkling wine, chilled

1 cup Riesling, chilled

2 navel oranges, thinly sliced

1 cup diced fresh pineapple (¼-inch dice)

½ cup pomegranate arils

GLASS: champagne flute or coupe, glass punch cup, or rocks

In a punch bowl, dissolve the sugar in the pomegranate juice. Add the champagne and the Riesling, then the orange slices, pineapple, and pomegranate arils. Serve over ice cubes.

RISE AND SHINE

"A cocktail is a work of art that dances on your taste buds."
—Unknown

Who does not look forward to the weekend? The weekend usually means brunch—a mini party that you treat yourself to on Saturday or Sunday mornings. You cannot have a proper brunch without a special cocktail to accompany that salmon and asparagus frittata, eggs Benedict, or red velvet waffles. Enjoy, my friends!

LILLET BURNT-ORANGE TWIST

Lillet is a French aperitif that has made a new home here in the South! A white or red version is available, and this is quite possibly the most versatile liqueur you can imagine. I think of it as an aperitif, but it works well as a light cocktail alternative, especially on an extremely warm Southern summer day. It is essentially a one-ingredient cocktail with a twist.

SERVES 1

White Lillet
Thick orange twist

GLASS: white wine

Fill the glass with ice and pour in the Lillet. Twist the orange zest, and, while holding it over the glass, light the tip of the twist with a match. Hold for a few seconds to allow the orange twist to start to burn and then drop it into the glass and submerge into the cocktail. This process releases the natural oils in the orange peel and intensifies the flavor experience.

APEROL BELLINI

A Bellini typically consists of peach purée with prosecco or sparkling wine—a simple two-ingredient wonder. This version of the peach-flavored drink is made a lot easier by substituting peach schnapps or brandy for the purée. The addition of Aperol, a sweet and bitter citrus liqueur, gives this cocktail its depth. It is simple yet elegant.

SERVES 1

1½ ounces peach liqueur
½ ounce Aperol
Prosecco or sparkling wine
Orange twist, for garnish

GLASS: champagne flute

Combine the peach liqueur and Aperol in the champagne flute, and top with prosecco. Garnish with a thin spiral of orange twist.

Lillet Burnt-Orange Twist

LOADED BLOODY MARY

The Bloody Mary is probably the most expressive cocktail—with so many ways to convey a singular idea. At its core, it is tomato juice and vodka. But what makes it exciting is all the ways to garnish it to enhance the experience. When serving a brunch crowd this is an easy make-ahead option.

SERVES 8 TO 10

6 cups tomato juice
2 tablespoons prepared horseradish
2 tablespoons lemon juice
1 tablespoon Worcestershire sauce
2 tablespoons celery salt, divided
1 tablespoon hot sauce
½ teaspoon fresh ground black pepper
1½ tablespoons kosher salt, divided
12 ounces vodka

OPTIONAL GARNISHES
Blue cheese–stuffed olives
Pickled okra
Poached shrimp
Pickled asparagus
Pickled string beans
Crispy strips of bacon
Celery ribs with leaves
Pepperoncini
Lemon wedges

GLASS: highball or collins

In a large pitcher, mix the tomato juice, horseradish, lemon juice, Worcestershire, 2 teaspoons celery salt, hot sauce, black pepper, ½ teaspoon kosher salt, and vodka. Cover and refrigerate. Mix the remaining celery salt and kosher salt together on a small plate. Dip the rim of the glasses in water, then into the celery salt mixture, and twist. Fill the glasses with ice and pour the cocktail mixture into glasses. Garnish as desired.

SPARKLING VODKA LEMONADE

Nothing is more Southern than lemonade. It is cool, refreshing, and easy to make. And one of the advantages of being an adult is that you can add vodka to it!

SERVES 1

4 ounces lemonade
2 ounces vodka
1 ounce limoncello (optional)
4 ounces club soda
Lemon wedge, for garnish
Fresh mint leaves and lemon wedge, for garnish

GLASS: collins

Fill a shaker halfway with ice and add the lemonade, vodka, and limoncello (if using). Shake to combine. Fill the glass with ice and pour in the lemonade. Top with club soda and garnish with the lemon wedge and mint.

MEGMOSA

Also known as a grapefruit mimosa, this delightful cocktail consisting of equal parts of sparkling wine and grapefruit juice is showing up on more Southern brunch menus.

SERVES 1

Sparkling wine (champagne, Crémant, prosecco, Cava) chilled
No-pulp grapefruit juice, chilled
Rosemary, mint, thyme, basil, or lavender sprigs, for garnish

GLASS: champagne flute

Fill the glass a little less than half full with chilled sparkling wine followed by the same amount of grapefruit juice. Add an herb sprig for a garnish.

Sparkling Vodka Lemonade

ABSINTHE-MINDED MARTINI

Illegal in the United States since 1912, absinthe made a strong comeback in 2007 when the ban was lifted. Absinthe, with its signature bitter anise-like flavor, is the cornerstone of the most popular cocktail in New Orleans, the Sazerac.

SERVES 1

½ ounce absinthe
3 ounces gin
½ ounce dry vermouth
½ ounce Grand Marnier
Orange peel, for garnish

GLASS: martini

In a shaker, combine ice, the absinthe, and gin and stir until chilled. Swirl the vermouth in the martini glass and pour out. Strain the drink into the glass and top with Grand Marnier. Garnish with the orange peel.

Negroni

NEGRONI

Considered an aperitif, the Negroni is rapidly becoming an "any time of day" cocktail. The Negroni consists of equal parts gin, sweet vermouth, and Campari. Try it as an alternative to juice-based brunch cocktails. When making this at home, choose your gin wisely—make sure it will hold up to the bold, bitter flavor of the Campari.

SERVES 1

1 ounce gin
1 ounce Campari
1 ounce sweet (red) vermouth
Orange wheel, for garnish

GLASS: rocks

Fill glass the with ice and add the gin, Campari, and vermouth. Stir well and garnish with the orange wheel.

PALOMA

The Paloma is a tequila, grapefruit, and lime juice cocktail; and is a cousin to the Greyhound cocktail, made with grapefruit juice and gin or vodka.

SERVES 1

Coarse sea salt, for rimming
Lime wedges, for rimming and garnish
2 ounces tequila
2 ounces grapefruit juice
½ ounce freshly squeezed lime juice
2 ounces sparkling water (Topo Chico, preferably)
Grapefruit wedge, for garnish

GLASS: rocks

Place the salt on a saucer. Rub the top edge of the glass with a wedge of lime and dip into salt. Pour the tequila, grapefruit juice, and lime juice into the glass and fill with ice. Top with sparkling water and garnish with lime and grapefruit wedges.

TENNESSEE ICED TEA

Many years of debate have gone into just where Long Island Iced Tea originated. Kingsport, Tennessee, claims that it was invented by Old Man Charles Bishop, who lived in Long Island in Kingsport during Prohibition in 1920. His original concoction blended five liquors, vodka, rum, gin, tequila, and whiskey, with maple syrup. In 1940 his son Ransom added cola and lemon and lime juice to the mix.

SERVES 1

1 ounce Tennessee whiskey
1 ounce tequila
1 ounce vodka
1 ounce light rum
1 ounce gin
1 ounce cane syrup
1 ounce freshly squeezed lemon juice
1 ounce freshly squeezed lime juice
Cola
Lemon slice, for garnish

GLASS: collins or hurricane

Fill a shaker with ice. Pour in the whiskey, tequila, vodka, rum, gin, cane syrup, lemon juice, and lime juice. Cover and shake until chilled. Pour into the glass and top off with cola. Garnish with the lemon slice.

ORANGE CRUSH

This cocktail with its multiple layers of orange flavoring is absolutely thirst-quenching! Do hand squeeze the orange juice for this recipe.

SERVES 1

2 ounces orange-flavored vodka

2 ounces Grand Marnier

2 ounces freshly squeezed orange juice

3 dashes orange bitters

Lemon-lime soda

Orange slices, for garnish

GLASS: rocks

Fill the glass with ice and pour in the vodka and Grand Marnier, orange juice, and bitters. Top with lemon-lime soda and garnish with the orange slices.

SWAMP WATER

The height of the popularity of the swamp water cocktail was the 1970s. I always loved the look and taste of this cocktail. Very mild and soothing, Chartreuse has many medicinal qualities. Developed by the Carthusian monks of France, it found its way to the United States as a cure for stomach ailments. To this day, I keep Chartreuse in my bar.

SERVES 1

1½ ounces green Chartreuse
4 ounces pineapple juice
½ ounce freshly squeezed lime juice
Pineapple wedge and pineapple leaves, for garnish
Lime wheel, for garnish

GLASS: collins or mason jar

Pour the Chartreuse, pineapple juice, and lime juice into the glass. Stir until combined. Garnish with the pineapple and lime.

PORCH SIPPIN'

"Here in the South, we don't hide crazy. We parade it on the front porch and give it a cocktail."
—Unknown

Nobody knows more about porch sittin' and sippin' than Southerners. In fact, we invented it and turned it into an art! Any time of the day, for no reason at all, this is how we roll. And because you are already at home, go ahead and try one of these bold cocktails made with local moonshine. You'll like it!

BLOOD ORANGE TEXAS MARGARITA

Not all margaritas are created equal! There is the traditional margarita made with tequila, orange liqueur, and lime juice. Then there is the Texas margarita, which has orange juice and agave nectar or simple syrup added.

SERVES 1

Fresh lime wedge
Coarse margarita salt, for rimming
2 ounces blanco tequila
1 ounce Grand Marnier, triple sec, or Cointreau
1 ounce freshly squeezed lime juice
1 ounce freshly squeezed blood orange juice
¼ ounce agave nectar
Blood orange slice, for garnish

GLASS: margarita or rocks

Wet the rim of the glass with the lime wedge and dip the glass rim into the salt. In a cocktail shaker, combine the tequila, Grand Marnier, lime juice, blood orange juice, and agave nectar. Shake until well blended. Strain into the glass and garnish with the blood orange slice.

BERRY AND PEACH SANGRIA

This cocktail takes advantage of summer's favorite fruit, the peach, and its most seasonal berries.

SERVES 8

1 bottle (750 milliliters) white wine (sauvignon blanc, pinot grigio, or Vermentino)

2 ounces orange liqueur (Grand Marnier, triple sec, or Cointreau)

2 peaches, peeled and sliced

1 lemon, sliced

1 lime, sliced

1 cup blackberries

1 cup strawberries, green tops removed, sliced

16 ounces club soda

Mint leaves, for garnish

GLASS: white wine or rocks

Combine the wine, liqueur, peaches, lemon, lime, and berries in a large pitcher. Cover and refrigerate until well chilled. When ready to serve, top with the club soda and stir well. Fill glasses with ice and pour in the sangria. Garnish with mint leaves.

MANGO COLADA

What happens when mango meets piña colada? Pure tropical bliss! I really like this cocktail, so I went a little heavy on the rum. If you prefer a lighter drink, you may want to reduce the amount of rum to 2 ounces.

SERVES 2

1 mango
4 ounces cream of coconut
4 ounces pineapple juice
4 ounces white rum
2 cups ice (or more, depending how thick you like it)
Pineapple triangles or pineapple leaves, for garnish

GLASS: hurricane or highball

Cut the mango in half. Chop one half into pieces and cut the other half into wedges for the garnish. Set aside the wedges.

Mix the cream of coconut, pineapple juice, rum, mango pieces, and ice in a blender until the mango is smooth. Pour into glasses and garnish with mango wedges and pineapple triangles or leaves.

COCONUT MOJITO

The mojito originated in Cuba. A cousin to the mint julep, it is made with rum instead of bourbon. The mojito is considered a warm-weather cocktail, which is why it has a strong following in the South. I prefer to use coconut rum in this cocktail in place of regular rum and crème of coconut.

SERVES 1

1 tablespoon fine lime zest

2 tablespoons plus 1 teaspoon superfine sugar, divided

6 mint leaves, torn (no stems)

½ ounce freshly squeezed lime juice

1 teaspoon superfine sugar

2 ounces coconut rum

4 ounces club soda

Fresh mint sprig, for garnish

Lime wheel, for garnish

GLASS: collins or highball

In a small shallow bowl, combine the lime zest and 2 tablespoons of the sugar. Wet the rim of the glass with lime juice or water and dip the glass rim in the lime sugar. In a cocktail shaker, combine the mint leaves, lime juice, and the remaining 1 teaspoon sugar. Muddle well to break up the leaves and extract the oils of the mint leaves. Add the rum and fill the shaker with ice. Shake until chilled. Strain into the glass and top off with the club soda. Garnish with the mint sprig and lime wheel.

AVIATION

No one can say for sure where this classic gin-based cocktail originated, only that it has been around since the early 1900s. And like most classic cocktails, it requires few ingredients. One such ingredient is the elusive crème de violette liqueur that gives the aviation its unique color. Absent for many years, it is in production and available again. Use top-shelf ingredients in this cocktail for the optimum drinking experience.

SERVES 1

2 ounces Aviation gin
1 ounce freshly squeezed lemon juice
¼ ounce crème de violette
¼ ounce Luxardo maraschino liqueur
Luxardo maraschino cherry, for garnish
Flamed lemon peel or edible violets, for garnish

GLASS: martini coupe or cocktail

In a shaker filled with ice, combine the gin, lemon juice, crème de violette, and maraschino liqueur. Shake until well chilled. Strain into the glass and garnish as desired.

CHEF B'S CITRUS-CHAMPAGNE SANGRIA

This crowd-pleasing bubbly and festive sangria is a party waiting to happen. Perfect for summer or anytime holidays, celebrations or just because. Make it yours and whatever you want it to be! Rosemary as a garnish with this cocktail holds its own with the powerful and fragrant citrus flavors.

MAKES 1 LARGE PITCHER

1 grapefruit
1 lemon
1 orange
1 large lime
¼ cup superfine sugar
¼ cup cognac
1 bottle (750 milliliters) red wine
½ cup orange juice
1 bottle (750 milliliters) champagne or prosecco
Fruit slices, for garnish
Rosemary sprigs, for garnish

GLASS: red wine or cooler

Thinly slice the grapefruit, orange, lemon, and lime. Place in a container and sprinkle with sugar and cognac. Cover and refrigerate at least 4 hours.

Put ice in a large pitcher (at least 60 ounces) and add the citrus mixture. Pour in the red wine, orange juice, and champagne. Stir to thoroughly combine. Pour into glasses filled with ice and garnish with fruit slices and rosemary.

1792 KENTUCKY WHITE DOG JULEP

"White dog" is one of the many terms used to describe moonshine. The difference between the white dog julep and the mint julep is the use of unaged corn liquor versus bourbon. Thus, the white dog julep is clear, and the mint julep is amber. The mojito, made with rum, is a close cousin.

SERVES 1

6 mint leaves
½ ounce Plain Simple Syrup (page 16)
2 ounces unaged clear corn whiskey (white dog)
Mint sprigs, for garnish

GLASS: highball or julep cup

Place the mint leaves and syrup in the glass. With a muddler, press the leaves gently until broken up. Add the whiskey and half pack the glass with crushed ice. Stir, then top off with more crushed ice. Garnish with two or three sprigs of fresh mint.

MOONSHINE LEMONADE

This lemonade packs quite a punch. I would recommend keeping this out of the reach of anyone who isn't of legal drinking age. Conversely, this might be just the thing to serve at your next adult cookout!

SERVES 1

1½ ounces corn whiskey
1 ounce Plain Simple Syrup (page 16)
Juice of 1 lemon
Club soda
1 lemon wedge, for garnish

GLASS: small mason jar or rocks

Pour the whiskey, simple syrup, and lemon juice into a shaker. Shake until well combined. Pour into the glass filled with ice and top with club soda. Garnish with the lemon wedge.

1792 Kentucky White Dog Julep

VODKA STRAWBERRY LEMONADE

So there I was, sitting at the bar in the Palm Restaurant in Charlotte, North Carolina. It happened to be very slow that Saturday evening, and the bartender, Andrew R., was unusually talkative. I mentioned that I was writing a book on Southern cocktails. That is when he offered up this enhanced lemonade recipe. I tested it and I liked it, so here you go. It is indeed a refreshing drink . . . especially for porch sippin'.

SERVES 1

2 ounces lemon vodka

½ ounce Lavender Simple Syrup (page 17)

2 ounces lemonade

¼ cup sliced strawberries

Prosecco or champagne (or lemon-lime soda for a nonalcoholic option)

Strawberry, cut half or sliced (with green leaf and stem
    still on top), for garnish

Lemon wheel, for garnish

GLASS: large rocks or highball

In a shaker, combine the vodka, simple syrup, lemonade, and strawberries. Muddle until the strawberries are softened. Strain into the glass and top with prosecco. Garnish with the strawberry and lemon wheel.

IN-THE-WOODS
MOONSHINE COCKTAIL

During the Civil War, a whiskey tax was introduced to help fund the govern-ment. The tax was so high that some distillers would hide in the woods to avoid paying the tax. Thus started the tradition of illegal, cheap liquor being made deep in the woods to escape the law and prosecution. And although the production of commercial moonshine is on the rise, there are still many making it the old-fashioned way, in the woods.

SERVES 1

2 ounces corn whiskey
2 ounces cranberry juice
2 ounces freshly squeezed orange juice
1 ounce peach schnapps
Orange and lime wheels, for garnish

GLASS: mason jar or highball

Pour the whiskey, cranberry juice, orange juice, and peach schnapps into the glass filled with ice. Stir until combined. Garnish with the citrus wheels.

ULTIMATE SOUTHERN-INSPIRED MARTINIS

"I would like to observe the vermouth from across the room while I drink my martini."
—Sir Winston Churchill

Unlike other cocktails, the martini has remained as simple and easy as it always has been. Two ingredients define the martini: gin (or vodka) and vermouth. And for the most part it has remained simple in nature. There have been many spin-offs and iterations of the martini, but they too have remained relatively unfussy, which must be why it is among the most popular cocktails in the world.

Martinis are also quite possibly the most controversial of all cocktails. Everyone who drinks them has a special preference for how they are to be made: gin or vodka, which brand of vodka or gin, how wet or dry it is, and what to use as a garnish. If you ask me, the argument came to a head when someone came up with the idea of floating an olive stuffed with blue cheese in a martini. Oh, and don't forget the issue of shaking versus stirring, but that's for another day . . .

Give the fact that you have thought about the above-mentioned questions, now you are ready to order your martini one of four ways:

Dry—a low ratio of vermouth

Extra dry—the slightest splash of vermouth or just washing the glass with the vermouth and discarding before the cocktail is poured into the glass

Wet—higher percentage of vermouth added to the gin or vodka

Dirty—the addition of olive juice

CHEERS!

CLASSIC MARTINI

The original and still classic version.

SERVES 1

2 ½ ounces gin or vodka
½ ounce dry vermouth
Lemon twist or olive, for garnish

GLASS: chilled martini

Pour the gin and vermouth into a mixing glass half-filled with ice. Stir until very cold. Strain into the chilled glass. Garnish with the lemon twist or olive.

LEMON DROP MARTINI

You might call this lemonade with vodka in it.

SERVES 1

Granulated sugar, for rimming
Lemon wedge
2 ½ ounces vodka
1 ½ ounces freshly squeezed lemon juice
1 ounce Plain Simple Syrup (page 16)
Lemon wheel, for garnish

GLASS: chilled martini

Put the sugar in a shallow bowl or saucer. Run the lemon wedge around the rim of the glass and dip the glass in sugar. Add the vodka, lemon juice, and simple syrup to a mixing glass half-filled with ice. Stir until very cold. Strain into the chilled glass. Garnish with the lemon wheel.

CHOCOLATE MARTINI

Who wouldn't like a chocolate martini? This recipe is made with Baileys Irish Cream and sprinkled with shaved chocolate.

SERVES 1

2 ounces Baileys Irish Cream
1 ounce crème de cacao
1 ounce vodka
Shaved or ground chocolate, for garnish

GLASS: chilled martini

In a shaker half-filled with ice, combine the Baileys, crème de cacao, and vodka. Shake until well chilled. Strain into the chilled glass. Garnish with the chocolate.

Dirty Cajun Martini

DIRTY CAJUN MARTINI

This recipe uses peppered vodka, a splash of Louisiana hot sauce, and olive brine.

SERVES 1

2 ½ ounces peppered vodka
½ ounce vermouth
¼ ounce olive brine
Dash Louisiana hot sauce
Half jalapeño pepper or green olives, for garnish

GLASS: chilled martini

Add the vodka, vermouth, olive brine, and hot sauce to a mixing glass half-filled with ice. Stir until very cold. Strain into the chilled glass. Garnish as desired.

PINEAPPLE MARTINI

This martini dances in your mouth! The secret here is the addition of Tuaca (an Italian brandy with citrus and vanilla undertones) and amaretto (an almond liqueur). I am already envisioning these ingredients in my next pound cake.

SERVES 1

1 ounce Tuaca
1 ounce amaretto
1 ounce vodka
1 ½ ounces pineapple juice
Pineapple wedge, for garnish

GLASS: chilled martini

In a shaker, combine the Tuaca, amaretto, vodka, and pineapple juice. Shake until well chilled. Pour into the chilled glass and garnish with the pineapple wedge.

SOUTHERN BELLE MARTINI

A martini made with quintessential Southern ingredients.

SERVES 1

1 ounce bourbon
1½ ounces Southern Comfort
1 ounce orange juice
½ ounce pineapple juice
Orange twist, for garnish

GLASS: chilled martini

In a shaker, combine the whiskeys and juices. Shake until well chilled. Pour into the chilled glass and garnish with orange twist.

PICKLETINI

If you are a huge fan of pickles and martinis, you are going be over the moon with this martini.

SERVES 1

2½ ounces Cathead Vodka
1 ounce pickle juice
Cornichons, for garnish
Olives, for garnish

GLASS: chilled martini

Pour the vodka and pickle juice into a mixing glass half-filled with ice. Stir until very cold. Strain into a chilled glass. Garnish with the cornichons and olives.

Southern Belle Martini

LILLETINI

Lillet (pronounced lee-LAY) is a French aromatic that is flexible enough to pair with any liquor or wine. Referred to as summer in a glass, *this Lilletini will be the perfect summer martini option.*

SERVES 1

2 ½ ounces vodka
½ ounce Lillet Blanc
2 to 3 dashes orange bitters
Orange twist, for garnish

GLASS: chilled martini

Pour the vodka, Lillet Blanc, and bitters into a mixing glass half-filled with ice. Stir until very cold. Strain into the chilled glass. Garnish with the orange twist.

ESPRESSO MARTINI

With our newfound obsession with specialty coffee, the espresso martini has replaced the Manhattan as one of the ten most ordered cocktails.

SERVES 1

2 ounces vodka
½ ounce coffee liqueur
2 ounces freshly brewed espresso
¼ ounce Plain Simple Syrup (page 16)
Chocolate sprinkles or coffee beans, for garnish

GLASS: chilled martini

Pour the vodka, coffee liqueur, espresso, and simple syrup into a shaker half-filled with ice. Shake until well chilled. Strain into the chilled glass. Garnish as desired.

PEPPERMINT MARTINI

Get into the holiday spirit with this candy cane–inspired martini.

SERVES 1

2 tablespoons white chocolate chips, melted
1 candy cane, crushed
2 ounces peppermint vodka
1 ounce white Irish cream
1 ounce heavy whipping cream
Small candy cane or peppermint, for garnish

GLASS: chilled martini

Place the melted chocolate in a shallow bowl or saucer. Place the crushed candy in another shallow bowl or saucer. Rim the glass first in the chocolate, then in the crushed candy. Refrigerate until ready to fill.

Pour the vodka, Irish cream, and whipping cream into a shaker half-filled with ice. Shake until well chilled. Strain into the chilled glass. Garnish with the candy cane.

FIVE O'CLOCK
SOMEWHERE

"Wine makes daily living easier,
less hurried, with fewer tensions,
and more tolerance."
—Benjamin Franklin

We all have a favorite wine or wines. You have probably gone as far as pairing them to your meals of preference. You do not have to be a wine connoisseur to enjoy these wine cocktails. Just add some simple ingredients that you already have in your home bar, or that can be easily sourced. Now you have just discovered another way to enjoy what you know you already like!

Kir Royale

KIR ROYALE

Kir is simply white wine and crème de cassis. To make a kir royale, use champagne or any sparkling wine instead of white wine.

SERVES 1

½ ounce crème de cassis
Champagne or sparkling wine
Blackberry or lemon twist, for garnish

GLASS: champagne flute

Pour the crème de cassis into the bottom of the glass. Top off with the champagne. Garnish with the blackberry.

TEQUILA SANGRIA

Sangria is a combination of red wine, fruit, fruit juices, liquor, liqueurs, and sweetener. Although it is traditionally made with red wine, it is rapidly becoming popular to see it made with white wine, rosé, and sparkling wines.

SERVES 12

¾ cup blanco tequila
¼ cup triple sec
4 cups fruity red wine
⅓ cup Plain Simple Syrup (page 16)
1½ cups orange juice
1 cup lime juice
1 to 2 cups sparkling water
Orange, lime, and lemon slices, for garnish

GLASS: red wine

Pour the tequila, triple sec, wine, simple syrup, and juices into a large pitcher or punch bowl. Stir until combined. When ready to serve, add the sparkling water and stir again. Add the fruit slices and ice to glasses and pour the sangria.

CAMPARI BICYCLE COCKTAIL

This drink is guaranteed to make you swerve on your bicycle if you drink too many.

SERVES 1

2 ounces Campari
2 ounces dry white wine
Club soda
Orange wheel, for garnish

GLASS: white wine

Pour the Campari and white wine into the glass filled with ice. Top with the club soda and stir. Garnish with the orange wheel.

BLACK VELVET

This recipe is said to have been inspired by Elvis Presley, whose image was often painted on black velvet fabric. This cocktail is made with Guinness stout and sparkling wine.

SERVES 1

Guinness stout, chilled
Champagne or sparkling wine, chilled

GLASS: highball

Fill the glass halfway with the Guinness. Top with the sparkling wine by pouring it over the back of a spoon.

Campari Bicycle Cocktail

Cardinal

CARDINAL

This is a take on the kir but with red wine instead of white.

SERVES 1

1 ounce crème de cassis
5 ounces dry red wine
3 blackberries, for garnish

GLASS: red wine

Pour the crème de cassis in the glass filled with ice. Top with the red wine. Garnish with the blackberries.

WINE SOUR

This is what happens when a whiskey sour meets red wine! This recipe updates the traditional whiskey sour by floating red wine on top.

SERVES 1

2 ounces bourbon
1 ounce lemon juice
¾ ounce Plain Simple Syrup (page 16)
½ ounce red wine

GLASS: rocks

In a shaker half-filled with ice, combine the bourbon, lemon juice, and simple syrup. Shake well. Strain into glass over a large square ice cube. Slowly pour the red wine over the back of a spoon so the wine floats on top of the drink.

BISHOP

This classic cocktail is a glass of red wine with rum, simple syrup, and lime juice.

SERVES 1

3 ounces rum
2 ounces red wine
½ ounce freshly squeezed lime juice
1 teaspoon Plain Simple Syrup (page 16)
Lime wheels, for garnish

GLASS: chilled red wine

Pour the rum, wine, lime juice, and simple syrup into a shaker half-filled with ice. Shake until well chilled. Pour into the chilled glass. Garnish with the lime wheels.

BERRY SLUSH

At the height of summer in the South it gets hot! And sometimes you just want something to cool you down fast. This can help . . .

SERVES 2

2 cups red, white, or rosé wine
¼ cup frozen raspberries
¼ cup frozen blackberries
¼ cup sliced frozen strawberries
1 tablespoon honey
Fresh berries and mint leaves, for garnish

GLASS: large rocks

Pour the wine into ice trays and freeze several hours to overnight.

Combine 3 regular ice cubes (depending on size) and 6 frozen wine ice cubes with the frozen berries and the honey in a blender. Pulse until well blended. Pour into the chilled glasses. Garnish with fresh berries and mint.

SPRITZES, SMASHES, AND FARTS

"Cocktails are a passport to explore new flavors and experiences."
—Unknown

There are some new cocktails that are becoming ever so popular on the cocktail scene. Many of them are made with liqueurs and aperitifs, enhanced with the addition of herbs and bitters, and finished with simple mixers like club soda, simple syrup, and juices. And some of these drinks are just a lot of fun.

Spritz

The spritz may have been born in Venice but its popularity has grown by leaps and bounds in the US South. Our longer warm seasons send us constantly in search of alternatives to the usual white wine and cold fruity summer cocktails.

Smash

A smash is an ancient cocktail template that dates to 1862. Technically a smash is a type of julep—a concoction of spirits, sugar, mint, ice, and fruit. But this rule is open to interpretation, because at its core the smash is a very forgiving and flexible drink. While in a traditional julep mint is the classic choice, many other herbs will work just as well.

Fart

A fart is simply a shot mixed with three ingredients. Most of the time the ingredients are layered, but not always. It was popularized by the Alaska Duck Fart created at the Peanut Farm, a small bar in Anchorage, Alaska. Today the fart is slowly working its way into mainstream bar culture in the Lower 48.

APEROL ROSÉ SPRITZ

Aperol is a bright orange bittersweet Italian aperitif that serves as the perfect mixer—its low alcohol content complements most cocktails.

SERVES 1

3 ounces prosecco rosé
2 ounces Aperol
1 ounce club soda
Lemon twist or orange wheel, for garnish

GLASS: wine

Fill the glass with ice and add the prosecco followed by the Aperol. Top with the club soda and garnish as desired.

CLASSIC CAMPARI SPRITZ

The Campari spritz, by comparison to the Aperol spritz, is higher in alcohol content and tastes more bitter. It is more herbal and less fruity than its counterpart. Some might find this version to be more refreshing on a hot day.

SERVES 1

3 ounces dry prosecco
2 ounces Campari
1 ounce club soda
Orange wheel, for garnish

GLASS: wine

Fill the glass with ice and add the prosecco followed by the Campari. Top with the club soda and garnish with the orange wheel.

Classic Campari Spritz (left) and Aperol Rosé Spritz (right)

RASPBERRY AND TARRAGON SMASH

This smash has layer upon layer of flavors, with the bourbon, tarragon, raspberries, and lime. The very slight hint of licorice taste in the tarragon is a perfect pairing to the lime in this drink.

SERVES 1

¼ cup raspberries, plus more for garnish
2 tarragon sprigs
1 teaspoon granulated sugar
2 dashes lime bitters
2 ounces bourbon
1 ounce lime juice
Edible flowers, for garnish (optional)

GLASS: rocks

Place ¼ cup raspberries, 1 tarragon sprig, sugar, and bitters in a shaker. Muddle until the berries are smashed and the tarragon leaves are bruised. Add crushed ice, the bourbon, and the lime juice. Shake until well chilled. Strain into the glass filled with ice. Garnish with raspberries, the other tarragon sprig, and the flowers (if using).

BOURBON SMASH

This is what happens when mint julep meets whiskey sour. Bourbon, mint, and citrus—simple to make and even easier to enjoy!

SERVES 1

6 to 8 mint leaves
¾ ounce Plain Simple Syrup (page 16)
½ lemon, cut into wedges
2 ounces bourbon
Mint sprig, for garnish
Blackberries, for garnish (optional)

GLASS: rocks

In a shaker, combine the mint leaves, simple syrup, and lemon wedges. Muddle until the mint and lemon wedges are bruised. Add the bourbon and ice and shake until well chilled. Strain into the glass filled with ice. Garnish with the mint sprig and the blackberries (if using).

DUCK FART

The original drink made with Kahlúa, Baileys, and whiskey.

SERVES 1

½ ounce Kahlúa
½ ounce Baileys
½ ounce whiskey

GLASS: shot

Pour the Kahlúa into the glass. Then, holding a spoon diagonally over the Kahlúa, slowly pour the Baileys into the glass across the back of the spoon. Using the same method, pour the whiskey over the Baileys. This should result in very distinct layers.

FART HEARD AROUND THE WORLD

This fart was developed by Justin Rankin, "Chef of the Bar" at the Katharine Brasserie + Bar in Winston-Salem, North Carolina. This recipe features liquors that are locally sourced from around the state. Damn Fine Coffee Liqueur is produced in Durham, Southern Star Double Shot Coffee Bourbon Cream is produced in Statesville, and Old Nick Williams Bourbon is produced in Lewisville.

SERVES 1

1 ounce Damn Fine Coffee Liqueur
1 ounce Southern Star Double Shot Coffee Bourbon Cream
1 ounce Old Nick Williams Bourbon

GLASS: large shot

Pour the coffee liqueur into the glass. Then, holding a spoon diagonally over the coffee liqueur, slowly pour the bourbon cream into the glass across the back of the spoon. Using the same method, pour the bourbon over the bourbon cream. Or enjoy the ingredients over ice.

MONKEY FART

A shot cocktail made with tequila, cinnamon schnapps, and Tabasco sauce.

SERVES 1

3 to 5 ounces Tabasco sauce
½ ounce gold tequila
½ ounce cinnamon schnapps

GLASS: shot

Pour the Tabasco into the glass. Then, holding a spoon diagonally over the Tabasco, slowly pour the tequila into the glass across the back of the spoon. Using the same method, pour the schnapps over the tequila.

ALLIGATOR FART

A tropical-flavored shot cocktail made with grenadine, Midori (melon liqueur), and Jägermeister.

SERVES 1

½ ounce grenadine
½ ounce Midori
½ ounce Jägermeister

GLASS: shot

Pour the grenadine into the glass. Then, holding a spoon diagonally over the grenadine, slowly pour the Midori into the glass across the back of the spoon. Using the same method, pour the Jägermeister over the Midori. This should result in very distinct layers.

SHANDIES AND
BEER COCKTAILS

"A fine beer may be judged
with only one sip, but it's better
to be thoroughly sure."
—Czech Proverb

A shandy is probably the simplest of all cocktails to
make! It requires very little measuring and is a combination of equal amounts of beer and lemon-lime soda or
other soft drinks such as ginger beer or ginger ale. Other

mixers include orange juice, grapefruit juice, and cider. The beers used to make the ideal shandy are pale ales, pilsners, or lagers. Dark beers and stouts are not customarily used to make shandies as they might overwhelm the citrus flavors of the cocktail. By region, the South consumes the most beer, which makes the shandy one of the most *Southern* of all cocktails!

A beer cocktail is made by mixing beer with other ingredients, such as tomato juice, lime juice, Worcestershire sauce, spices, another lighter beer, and sometimes a type of liquor. While very similar to a shandy, the beer cocktails will contain mostly beer, whereas the shandy will have a higher mixer ingredient content.

CLASSIC SHANDY

The classic shandy is simply beer with a lemon-based mixer.

SERVES 1

6 ounces chilled beer
6 ounces chilled lemon-lime soda
Lemon or lime slice, for garnish

GLASS: tall beer glass or mason jar

Pour the beer into the glass, being careful to tilt the glass while pouring the beer. Then follow with the lemon-lime soda. Be sure to start with cold beer and soda, as using ice can dilute the cocktail—therefore the taste—before you have finished consuming it. Garnish with the citrus slice.

GINGER SHANDY

This shandy dates back to Victorian England and is the precursor to ginger beer.

SERVES 1

4 pieces crystallized ginger
1 cup sugar
Lemon wedge
8 ounces chilled lager beer
8 ounces chilled ginger ale or ginger beer
Fresh mint sprigs, for garnish

GLASS: tall beer

In a mini food processor, blitz the ginger and sugar until completely granulated. Place the mixture into a shallow bowl. Squeeze and rub the lemon wedge around the rim of the glass then twirl the rim in the ginger sugar. Carefully combine the beer and ginger ale in the glass and stir. Garnish with the mint sprigs.

CAMPARI SHANDY

The Campari in this shandy adds a bitter taste to the citrusy flavors of the drink.

SERVES 1

2 ounces Campari
1 ounce lime juice
12 ounces chilled IPA
Lime wedge, for garnish

GLASS: tall beer

Pour the Campari and the lime juice into the glass, followed by the beer. Stir gently. Garnish with the lime wedge.

South-of-the-
Border Shandy

SOUTH-OF-THE-BORDER SHANDY

This shandy is made with Mexican beer with some chili powder added for added spice.

MAKES 1 (64-OUNCE) PITCHER

24 ounces chilled Corona beer
24 ounces chilled lemon-lime soda
16 ounces chilled mango juice
4 ounces ancho chili powder
4 teaspoon kosher salt
Lime wheels or wedges, for garnish

GLASS: tall beer

In a ½-gallon pitcher, preferably one with a lid, combine the beer, soda, and mango juice. Cover and keep chilled until ready to serve. In a small bowl, combine the chili powder and salt. Pour into a shallow bowl and set aside. When ready to serve, moisten the rims of the serving glasses with water and twirl in the spiced salt, then fill with the shandy. Garnish with lime wheels.

CHELADA BEER COCKTAIL

A very simple Mexican beer cocktail consisting of beer and lime juice. This refreshing cocktail is your new go-to for a lazy weekend brunch.

SERVES 1

Lime wedges, for rimming and garnish
Tajín chili lime rimming salt
12 ounces Mexican beer
1 ounce freshly squeezed lime juice

GLASS: tall beer or highball

Swipe a lime wedge around the top edge of the glass. Dip the glass edge in the rimming salt. Fill the glass with ice and add the beer and lime juice. Stir gently. Garnish with a lime wedge.

PALOMA BEER COCKTAIL

A paloma is a light refreshing drink that combines citrus, beer, and tequila into one cocktail. Leave out the beer—ginger beer or a regular beer—and you almost end up with a hybrid form of margarita.

SERVES 1

2 ounces tequila
3 ounces freshly squeezed grapefruit juice
½ ounce Plain Simple Syrup (page 16)
Rimming salt
6 ounces ginger beer
¼ slice grapefruit, for garnish
Rosemary sprig, for garnish

GLASS: tall beer or highball

Combine the tequila, grapefruit juice, and simple syrup in a cocktail shaker. Rim the glass with the salt. Add ice to the glass and to the cocktail shaker. Seal the shaker and shake vigorously. Pour through a strainer into the ice-filled glass and top with the ginger beer. Garnish with the grapefruit slice and rosemary sprig.

Southern Mule

SOUTHERN MULE

A mule is a cocktail made with vodka, ginger beer, and lime, served in a copper mug. This Southern mule is made with Cathead Vodka from Mississippi and Wild Ginger ginger beer made in Tennessee.

SERVES 1

2 ounces Cathead Honeysuckle Vodka
¼ lime
4 ounces Wild Ginger ginger beer
Fresh mint, lime wheels, and edible wild flowers, for garnish

GLASS: copper mug

Fill the copper cup with crushed ice. Add the vodka, squeeze in the lime juice, and drop the lime into the cup. Top with the ginger beer and garnish as desired.

BLACK AND TAN

A black and tan is a mixture of two beers, a lighter ale and a dark stout. The lighter ale serves as the base of the drink while the darker stout is floated on the top. Black and tans are typically made with Bass Ale and Guinness stout; however, Bass Ale has been discontinued, and pale ales and lagers are now a good substitute. The key to layering is to use the back of a spoon and slowly pour the dark layer so that the two layers and colors remain separated.

SERVES 1

8 ounces Harp Lager or pale ale beer
8 ounces Guinness stout

GLASS: 16-ounce American pint glass (this glass is wider at the mouth than the base) or 20-ounce imperial glass

Pour the light lager into the glass. If it forms foam on top, that will help with the layering. Slowly pour the stout over back of a spoon to fill the glass and then serve.

PANACHÉ (FRENCH SHANDY)

This is a French version of the classic shandy, with the use of lemonade in place of the lemon-lime soda.

SERVES 1

8 ounces cold lager
4 to 8 ounces cold sparkling lemonade or lemon-lime soda
Thin lemon wheel, for garnish

GLASS: tall beer glass

Pour the lager into the glass. Add the sparkling lemonade or lemon-lime soda according to your taste preference. Float the lemon wheel on top of the cocktail.

ALMOST COCKTAILS

"Cocktails are conversation in a glass."
—Unknown

These are not the Shirley Temple drinks of your youth. There will be occasions when you may want the flavor of a cocktail without the alcohol. This is when a mocktail will fit the bill. No more having to explain to everyone why you choose to forego the alcohol for any given reason. You will be pleasantly surprised to know that all of these mocktails taste good with or without the addition of alcohol.

CHERRY-LIME RICKEY

The perfect combo of sweet, tart, and nonalcoholic refreshment.

SERVES 1

½ cup tart cherry juice
1 ounce freshly squeezed lime juice
½ ounce Plain Simple Syrup (page 16)
Club soda
Lime wedge, for garnish
Fresh cherries, for garnish

GLASS: highball

Fill the glass with ice and pour in the cherry juice, lime juice, and simple syrup. Top with the club soda and stir. Garnish with the lime wedge and cherries.

POMEGRANATE PALOMA

This mocktail is perfect for the holiday season. It is bright, cheery, tart, and sparkling.

SERVES 1

3 ounces pomegranate juice
1 ounce freshly squeezed orange juice
1 ounce freshly squeezed lime juice
4 ounces club soda
Rosemary sprig, for garnish
Orange wedge, for garnish

GLASS: highball or collins

Fill the glass with ice and pour in the pomegranate juice, orange juice, and lime juice. Top with the club soda and stir. Garnish with the rosemary sprig and orange wedge.

Cherry Lime Rickey

Sparkling Blueberry Lemonade

SPARKLING BLUEBERRY LEMONADE

Made from fresh sweet blueberries and tangy lemon, this drink is just what you need to quench your thirst during the heat of summer.

SERVES 2

1½ cups blueberries
Juice of 2 lemons
½ cup cold water
1½ cups cold sparkling water
3 tablespoons honey
Lemon slices, for garnish
Blueberries, for garnish

GLASS: highball

In a blender, combine the blueberries, lemon juice, and the cold water. Blend until smooth. Strain the mixture through a sieve, using the back of a wooden spoon to press any remaining solids through. Stir in the sparkling water and honey. Pour into 2 glasses filled with ice. Garnish with lemon slices and blueberries.

PINEAPPLE CITRUS TROPICAL

A three-ingredient mocktail of refreshing pineapple juice with an infusion of grapefruit-flavored water.

SERVES 1

3 ounces pineapple juice
6 ounces grapefruit sparkling water
Raspberries, for garnish

GLASS: highball

Fill the glass with ice and pour in the pineapple juice. Top with the grapefruit sparkling water and stir. Garnish with the raspberries.

BERRY FIZZ

A refreshing nonalcoholic beverage that you can share with adults and younger guests and family.

SERVES 1

1 cup mixed berries
2 ounces cranberry juice
1 ounce lime juice
Sparkling water
Lime wedge, for garnish

GLASS: highball or collins

Place the berries in a shaker and muddle until they are all broken. Add the cranberry juice and lime juice and fill the shaker with ice. Shake until well chilled. Strain into the glass filled with ice. Top with the sparkling water and stir. Garnish with the lime wedge.

PINEAPPLE GINGER BEER

This is the mocktail that will keep you coming back over and over again.

SERVES 1

6 mint leaves
1 ounce freshly squeezed lime juice
3 ounces pineapple juice
4 ounces nonalcoholic ginger beer
Lime wedge, mint sprig, or raspberries, for garnish

GLASS: rocks

Combine the mint and lime juice in a shaker. Muddle until the mint is bruised. Add the pineapple juice and shake vigorously. Fill the glass with ice and pour in the pineapple mixture. Top with the ginger beer. Garnish as desired.

WATERMELON SPRITZ

Watermelon is about as refreshing as it gets in the summertime.

SERVES 2

4 cups fresh seedless watermelon, cut into small chunks
5 mint leaves
2 tablespoons freshly squeezed lime juice
1½ tablespoons honey
Club soda
Lime wheels, for garnish
Mint sprigs, for garnish

GLASS: highball

In a blender, combine the watermelon, mint, lime juice, and honey. Blend until smooth. Fill the glasses with ice and strain the watermelon mixture into the glasses. Top with the club soda. Garnish with the lime wheels and mint sprigs.

GINGER-HONEY LEMONADE

Lemonade—a Southern thing! It is what makes summer perfect.

SERVES 4

1½ cups freshly squeezed lemon juice
4 cups water
¾ cup Spiced-Honey Syrup (page 18)
Fresh mint leaves, for garnish
Lemon wheels, for garnish

GLASS: highball

In a pitcher, combine the lemon juice, water, and honey syrup. Stir and taste; add more syrup if necessary. Add ice to the glasses and pour in the lemonade. Garnish with the mint leaves and lemon wheels.

Watermelon Spritz

CLASSIC SOUTHERN COCKTAILS

"A well-made cocktail is an invitation to indulge in life's pleasures."

—Unknown

Here are some truly Southern cocktails that may not be well-known to you but have been around and stood the test of time. At your next event it might be worth your effort to introduce or reintroduce one or more of these to your guests!

SOUTHERN GENTLEMAN

Move over, mint julep—there is a new Southern gentleman in town! Made with bourbon, rye, or Tennessee whiskey, this cocktail consists of simple syrup, mint, and blackberries with a little prosecco floated on top. This just might have you rethinking your drink of choice.

SERVES 1

1 ounce Plain Simple Syrup (page 16), chilled
5 fresh mint leaves, torn
5 fresh blackberries, plus extra for garnish
1½ ounces bourbon
Splash chilled prosecco
Mint sprig, for garnish

GLASS: rocks

In a shaker, combine the simple syrup, mint, and blackberries. Muddle until the mint and berries are bruised. Add the bourbon and shake well. Strain into the glass filled with crushed ice. Float a splash of chilled prosecco on top. Garnish with blackberries and the mint sprig.

MISSISSIPPI BOURBON PUNCH

Nowhere in the South is the muscadine grape more revered than in Missis-sippi. And muscadine wine forms the foundation for this Mississippi bourbon punch, with the addition of grenadine, bourbon, and fruit juices. Muscadines are truly the grape of the South. And this festive punch will be the star of your next gathering.

MAKES ABOUT 14 CUPS

2 bottles (750 milliliters each) dry muscadine wine, chilled
12 ounces grenadine, chilled
1½ cups bourbon, chilled
1 cup freshly squeezed orange juice, chilled
1 cup cranberry juice, chilled
⅓ cup freshly squeezed lime juice, chilled
12 ounces lemon-lime soda, chilled
1 cup club soda, chilled
Orange slices, for garnish
Lime slices, for garnish
Red and green muscadine grape halves, for garnish
Ice Mold, optional

ICE MOLD
1 small orange
1 lime
½ cup fresh cranberries
½ cup muscadine grapes
¼ cup cranberry juice
¾ cup water (more if needed to cover fruit)

GLASS: punch cups

In a large punch bowl, combine the wine, grenadine, bourbon, orange juice, cranberry juice, and lime juice. Cover and refrigerate. When you are ready to serve, stir in the lemon-lime soda and club soda and garnish with the orange and lime slices and grapes. Gently add the ice mold, if using.

For ice mold: Thinly slice the orange and lime into wheels and set aside. In the bottom of a 7-inch copper mold or Bundt pan, arrange the cranberries and muscadine grapes. Layer the orange and lime slices on top. In a medium pitcher, stir together the cranberry juice and water. Pour enough liquid into the mold to cover the fruit. Freeze overnight. To unmold, place the bottom of mold in slightly warm water for 2 to 3 minutes; just long enough to see the ice melting around the edges. Remove ice ring from pan and place in the punch bowl upside down—with berries and grapes on top.

RUM RUNNER

A combination of rum, banana liqueur, blackberry liqueur, grenadine, and tropical fruit juices, the Rum Runner gets its name from the Prohibition era and the smugglers in the Florida Keys who played a major role in transporting rum from the Bahamas to Florida's speakeasies.

SERVES 1

1 ounce light rum
1 ounce dark spiced rum
1 ounce banana liqueur (Banane du Brésil)
½ ounce blackberry liqueur
2 ounces pineapple juice
1 ounce lime juice
½ ounce grenadine
Maraschino cherry, for garnish
Pineapple wedge, for garnish

GLASS: hurricane

Combine the rums, banana liqueur, blackberry liqueur, pineapple juice, lime juice, and grenadine in a shaker. Add ice and shake until chilled. Fill the glass with crushed ice and strain drink into the glass. Garnish with the cherry and pineapple wedge.

BUSHWACKER

The easiest way to describe this cocktail made of ingredients like rum, Kahlúa, crème de cacao, and vanilla ice cream is to call it a boozy milkshake. Everyone has their own recipe—there really is no wrong way to make it. Originally developed on the island of Saint Thomas in the Caribbean, today this drink is extremely popular in the southeastern United States, especially in the panhandle of Florida. It got its name because two of the first customers to try it had their dog, named Bushwack, with them in the Virgin Islands. Since the bartender didn't have a name for this new concoction yet, she decided to name it after the dog! Every year the Bushwacker Festival is held in Pensacola.

SERVES 4

4 ounces crème of coconut
2 ounces Kahlúa
2 ounces Irish cream liqueur
2 ounces crème de cacao
2 ounces dark rum
1 ounce chocolate sauce or syrup
4 cups vanilla ice cream
Whipped cream, for garnish (optional)
Freshly grated nutmeg, for garnish
Maraschino cherry, for garnish

GLASS: hurricane

Place 3 cups of ice in a blender. Add the crème of coconut, Kahlúa, Irish cream, crème de cacao, rum, and chocolate sauce. Cover and process until the ice is finely chopped. Add the ice cream and process until smooth. Pour into glasses and garnish as desired.

VIEUX CARRÉ

Referred to as New Orleans in a glass, the Vieux Carré was invented at the legendary Carousel Bar. This drink's name means "old square," referring to New Orleans' French Quarter. This cocktail packs a powerful punch as it features several strong ingredients in one drink that produce flavors that range from boozy and bitter to smooth and sweet.

SERVES 1

¾ ounce rye whiskey
¾ ounce cognac
¾ ounce sweet vermouth
⅓ ounce Bénédictine liqueur
2 dashes Peychaud bitters
1 dash Angostura bitters
Lemon zest twist, for garnish

GLASS: rocks

Scoop some ice into a mixing glass and add the rye, cognac, vermouth, Bénédictine, and bitters. Stir until well chilled. Strain into the glass filled with ice. Garnish with the lemon twist.

Pimm's Cup

PIMM'S CUP

This gin cocktail was created in London but gained fame in New Orleans more than 100 years ago at the Napoleon House. Essentially it contains three ingredients: gin, lemonade, and 7 Up. This light cocktail can be enjoyed year-round. The Pimm's Cup pairs perfectly with a muffuletta, also a creation of Napoleon House.

SERVES 1

1¼ ounces Pimm's No.1 gin
3 ounces lemonade
7 Up
Sliced strawberry, orange wedge, mint sprig, and
cucumber slices, for garnish

GLASS: collins

Fill the glass with ice. Add the gin and lemonade. Top with the 7 Up and stir. Garnish as desired.

TEXAS RANCH WATER

A lower-calorie option to the margarita, this drink has just three ingredients: tequila, lime juice, and sparkling water. If you are low carb or keto, this drink is for you.

SERVES 1

2 ounces blanco tequila
1½ ounces freshly squeezed lime juice
Topo Chico Sparkling Mineral Water
Lime wedge, for garnish

GLASS: rocks

Fill the glass with ice. Pour in the tequila and lime juice. Top with Topo Chico. Garnish with the lime wedge.

SWEET TEA MULE

We Southerners always have a batch of sweet iced tea on hand, so adding a little booze to an already good drink can only make it better. And if vodka, ginger beer, and limes are staples for you, then you're always ready for a party that is just about ready to break out. You can make just one, but this recipe is very easy to make in a big batch.

SERVES 1

2 ounces prepared sweet iced tea
1 ounce vodka
¾ ounce freshly squeezed lime juice
3 ounces ginger beer
Fresh mint, for garnish
Lime wedge, for garnish

GLASS: copper mug

Fill the mug with crushed ice. Add the sweet tea, vodka, and lime juice. Top with the ginger beer. Garnish with the mint and lime wedge.

BRANDY MILK PUNCH

A recipe that combines milk with simple syrup, vanilla extract, nutmeg, and a variety of spirits like brandy, bourbon, and rum shows why New Orleans is the cocktail capital of the United States. The milk punch dates all the way back to the 1600s. And yet visitors and residents alike contribute to keeping this centuries-old cocktail on some of the finest menus in the Crescent City. This is something worth celebrating . . . a cocktail that goes from day to night without skipping a beat.

SERVES 1

2 ounces brandy or bourbon
2 teaspoons Plain Simple Syrup (page 16)
2 dashes vanilla extract
2 ounces whole milk
2 ounces half-and-half
Freshly grated nutmeg, for garnish
Cinnamon stick, for garnish (optional)

GLASS: highball

Combine the bourbon, simple syrup, vanilla, milk, and half-and-half in a shaker filled with ice. Shake until chilled. Strain into the glass filled with ice. Garnish sparingly with the nutmeg and add the cinnamon stick (if using).

BEE'S KNEES

As the name suggests, this drink that incorporates honey syrup is incredible, as well as being refreshing and easy to make.

SERVES 1

2 ounces gin
¾ ounce freshly squeezed lemon juice
½ ounce Spiced-Honey Syrup (page 18)
Lemon slices or twist, for garnish
Edible flowers and herbs, for garnish (optional)

GLASS: chilled cocktail

In a shaker filled with ice, combine the gin, lemon juice, and honey syrup. Shake until well chilled. Strain into the glass. Garnish as desired.

THE CHEER MAKER

Cheerwine is a uniquely Southern soft drink made in North Carolina for more than 100 years; and yet it is barely known outside of the state. Sort of a cross between Dr Pepper and Cherry Coke, it is quite refreshing and pairs well in alcoholic cocktails.

SERVES 1

2 ounces bourbon
Cheerwine
Lime wedge

GLASS: mason jar

Pour the bourbon into the glass filled with ice, and top off with the Cheerwine. Squeeze the lime juice into the glass and drop in the wedge.

Bee's Knees

NIBBLES AND BITES

"A cocktail is a timeless expression of hospitality and enjoyment."
—Unknown

We are talking about Southern hospitality here. No Southern host would ever invite you to their home without serving you a *nibble* to go along with that cocktail! *It's just not Southernly!*

CRAB HUSH PUPPIES

Now there is something that all Southerners know about, and that is hush puppies. Add crabmeat, and you've got a treat made in Southern heaven.

MAKES 12 TO 16

1 cup yellow cornmeal
¼ cup all-purpose flour
1½ teaspoons baking powder
½ teaspoon kosher salt
1 large egg, lightly beaten
¾ cup milk
½ small onion or shallot, finely chopped
½ cup lump crabmeat
½ cup corn kernels (optional)
Canola oil, for frying

In a large bowl, combine the cornmeal, flour, baking powder, and salt. In a separate bowl, whisk the egg, milk, and onion together, then add to the dry ingredients just until combined. Fold in the crabmeat and corn (if using).

In a deep skillet or Dutch oven, heat oil to 365 degrees F. Using a #60 cookie scoop or a tablespoon, drop the batter into the oil. Fry 2 to 2½ minutes or until golden brown. They will float when done. Drain on paper towels. Serve warm.

MAC AND CHEESE POPPERS

These appetizers can serve as the guest of honor at the dinner table or be the belle of the ball at your next cocktail party. The one thing we can all agree on is that we never tire of eating mac and cheese in whatever form!

MAKES 24

2 tablespoons unsalted butter
2 tablespoons all-purpose flour
1 cup milk
1½ cups half-and-half
Pinch nutmeg
½ teaspoon kosher salt
⅛ cayenne pepper
2 cups shredded cheddar cheese
8 ounces elbow macaroni, cooked according to instructions
¼ cup grated Parmesan cheese
¼ cup breadcrumbs
Crispy bacon bits, for garnish
Chopped fresh chives, for garnish

Preheat the oven to 350 degrees F. Spray a 24-cup mini muffin pan with nonstick cooking spray.

In a large saucepan over medium heat, melt the butter, then add the flour. Cook, stirring constantly, for about 3 minutes—do not let brown. Stir in the milk and half-and-half and whisk until mixture is smooth. Continue cooking, stirring constantly, until the mixture thickens. Add the nutmeg, salt, and cayenne pepper. Remove from the heat, add the cheddar cheese, and stir until the cheese is melted and the mixture is smooth. Add the pasta to the cheese mixture and stir until well combined.

Using a small scoop or tablespoon, portion the pasta into the muffin pan cups. In a small bowl, combine the Parmesan and breadcrumbs, and then sprinkle on top of the pasta. Bake for 15 to 20 minutes, until bubbly and slightly browned on top. Remove from the oven and let cool in the muffin pan for 10 minutes. Carefully remove to a serving plate. Garnish with bacon bits and chives.

CAVIAR DEVILED QUAIL EGGS

These unique deviled eggs require dainty handling, as you can eat them in a single bite! You will be pleasantly surprised by their creamier and slightly richer taste when compared to chicken eggs. A subtle touch of caviar is all you need to take these to the next level!

MAKES 24

12 quail eggs
2 tablespoons white vinegar, divided
2 tablespoons Duke's mayonnaise
1 teaspoon yellow mustard
2 dashes Tabasco sauce
Kosher salt
Coarsely ground black pepper
1 tablespoon small caviar
Paprika, for garnish
Capers, for garnish (optional)
Freshly chopped dill, for garnish

Place the quail eggs in a medium saucepan with water to cover and ½ teaspoon of the vinegar. Bring to a boil and cook for 5 minutes. Pour off the water and transfer the eggs to a large bowl filled with ice water. When the eggs are completely cooled, peel. (If you are able to refrigerate them overnight, the eggs will be easier to peel.) Cut in half lengthwise and remove the yolks.

In a small bowl, mash the yolks until smooth. Add the mayonnaise, mustard, Tabasco, the remaining vinegar, salt, and pepper and mix until thoroughly combined. Fold in the caviar. Place the mixture in a piping bag or small ziplock bag and cut off a corner of the bag. Pipe the contents into the egg halves. Arrange on a serving tray, sprinkle with paprika, and top each with a caper (if using). Garnish with dill and refrigerate until ready to serve.

SAUSAGE ROLL POPPERS

It is easy to make these sausage rolls from scratch, but it gets significantly easier if you buy the links and roll them in the pastry. And don't stop with Italian sausage—you can make these with andouille, kielbasa, and even hot dogs!

MAKES 36

1 pound Italian bulk sausage
2 large eggs
½ cup seasoned breadcrumbs
2 tablespoons freshly chopped parsley
1 tablespoon freshly chopped thyme
1 teaspoon garlic powder
1 teaspoon onion powder
½ teaspoon kosher salt
¼ teaspoon freshly ground black pepper
1 box (2 sheets) puff pastry, thawed
Dijon or spicy brown mustard, for serving

Preheat the oven to 400 degrees F. Line a large baking sheet with parchment paper and set aside. In a large bowl, mix together the sausage, 1 egg, breadcrumbs, parsley, thyme, garlic powder, onion powder, salt, and pepper. Divide the meat mixture into 6 equal portions and set aside.

Unfold both pastry pieces onto a floured surface and gently roll out until a little thinner and smooth on top. Cut each pastry dough into 3 long sections of equal size. Place sausage portions down the middle of each of the 6 dough pieces, leaving about an inch on both sides. Roll one side of the dough up and over the sausage; on the other side, brush with water and finish folding dough over, ending with the seam side down. Repeat until done rolling remaining sausage and dough.

Cut each log into 6 equal parts and place on the prepared baking sheet about 2 inches apart. Using a paring knife, lightly pierce the top of each piece to create venting holes. In a small bowl, whisk the remaining egg with 1 tablespoon water; brush on the tops and sides of the sausage rolls. Bake for 20 minutes until pastry is puffed and tops are golden brown.

Plate and serve with mustard.

MINI SHRIMP CAKES

These shrimp cakes are a pleasant and less expensive alternative to crab cakes. Serve with an easy lemon mayonnaise.

MAKES 20 TO 24

5 tablespoons butter, divided
4 tablespoons olive oil, divided
¾ cup chopped green onion
½ cup chopped red bell pepper
½ cup chopped celery
1 large garlic clove, minced
½ cup chopped fresh parsley
1 cup breadcrumbs
⅓ cup heavy cream
1 medium potato, boiled and mashed
Zest of 1 lemon
2 tablespoons fresh lemon juice
1 tablespoon Dijon mustard
½ teaspoon kosher salt
¼ teaspoon cayenne or crushed red pepper flakes
1 pound small shrimp, chopped
2 tablespoons unsalted butter, more as needed
2 tablespoons olive oil, more as needed
⅓ cup mayonnaise
3 teaspoons freshly squeezed lemon juice

In a skillet over medium heat, heat 3 tablespoons of the butter and 2 table-spoons of the oil. Sauté the onion, bell pepper, celery, and garlic until soft. Set aside to cool. In a large bowl, mix together the parsley, breadcrumbs, cream, potato, lemon zest, lemon juice, mustard, salt, and cayenne.

Combine the sautéed vegetables with the shrimp meat and the potato mixture and thoroughly combine. Cover and chill for 30 minutes. Shape into 20 to 24 cakes. Heat the remaining butter and olive oil in a large pan over medium heat. Cook the shrimp cakes for 4 to 5 minutes on each side until brown. Drain on a paper towel–lined plate. Keep warm until ready to serve.

In a small bowl, combine the mayonnaise and lemon juice. Serve with the shrimp cakes.

PIMENTO CHEESE AND
TOMATO SLIDERS

Pimento cheese goes straight to the heart of Southern food traditions, right down to the use of Duke's mayonnaise in the recipe. Not only does it just taste good, but you can also make just about everything with it, from omelets and baked potatoes to quesadillas and sandwiches.

MAKES 8 SLIDERS

2 cups shredded extra-sharp cheddar cheese (shred by hand or
   in a food processor; do not used pre-shredded cheese)
8 ounces cream cheese, softened
½ cup Duke's mayonnaise
1 (4-ounce) jar of pimientos, drained and chopped
¼ teaspoon garlic powder
1 small jalapeño, minced
8 slider buns
2 to 3 medium Roma tomatoes, sliced
Dill pickle slices (optional)
Freshly ground black pepper (optional)

Place the cheeses, mayonnaise, pimientos, garlic powder, and jalapeño in a food processor and pulse until well combined, but still a little chunky. Refrigerate until ready to assemble sandwiches, or at least 1 hour.

To serve, slice buns in half and add a scoop of pimento cheese on the bottom half of the buns. Top with a slice of tomato and a pickle slice and pepper (if using), and cover with the top of the bun. Hold together with 4-inch skewers for serving.

CRAB AND ARTICHOKE DIP

Whether served at a cocktail party or as the beginning of a celebratory meal, this appetizer is guaranteed to please! This is also a great vegetarian option. Make the pita points yourself or purchase them; it does not alter the success of this dish. Feel free to scale this recipe if you need to serve fewer people.

SERVES 10 TO 12

4 ounces Neufchâtel, softened
½ cup full-fat sour cream
7 ounces artichoke hearts, drained and chopped
1 large garlic clove, minced
Zest of 1 lemon
Kosher salt
Freshly ground black pepper
¼ cup shredded mozzarella cheese
¼ cup grated Parmesan cheese, plus more for topping
¼ cup chopped scallions
Pinch cayenne pepper
8 ounces lump crabmeat, drained and any shells removed
¼ cup finely chopped red bell pepper, for garnish
Chopped scallions, green tops only, for garnish
Homemade Pita Chips, for serving (page 133)
Celery sticks, for serving (optional)

Preheat the oven to 350 degrees F. In a large bowl, mix the Neufchâtel, sour cream, and artichokes until thoroughly combined. Add the garlic, lemon zest, salt, pepper, mozzarella, Parmesan, scallions, and cayenne. Mix until well blended. Add the crabmeat and mix gently—do not break up crab lumps.

Spread into a cast-iron skillet or baking dish sprayed with nonstick cooking spray. Sprinkle with additional grated Parmesan cheese, if desired. Bake for 25 to 30 minutes, until bubbly. Turn on the broiler and broil about 3 minutes, until lightly brown. Watch closely to avoid burning.

Remove from the oven and allow to cool for 10 to 15 minutes. Serve with pita chips and celery sticks (if using).

Homemade Pita Chips

¼ cup olive oil
Mediterranean spice blend
3 pita bread rounds

Preheat the oven to 400 degrees F. In a small bowl, mix the oil and spice blend. Using a food brush, brush the pita on both sides generously with the oil mixture. Cut the pita rounds into 6 or 8 wedges each. Place wedges on a baking sheet. Bake 5 to 10 minutes until crispy and golden brown. Let cool completely on the baking sheet.

APPLE BUTTER AND BRIE TARTLETS

Brie is naturally mild, buttery, and nutty in flavor. The hints of cinnamon and cloves in the apple butter makes these two ingredients the perfect combination.

MAKES 24

1 sheet puff pastry, thawed
5 ounces Brie cheese
½ cup apple butter
¼ cup chopped pecans

Preheat the oven to 400 degrees F. Grease a 24-cup mini muffin pan.

Press the seams of the puff pastry sheet together. Cut the sheets into quarters, then each quarter into 6 pieces. Use a rolling pin to flatten each piece of pastry into a square. Place 1 square into each muffin cup.

Put ½ teaspoon Brie, 1 teaspoon apple butter, and about ½ teaspoon chopped pecans into each muffin cup. Bake for 13 to 15 minutes, until golden brown. Serve warm.

MINI HOT BROWNS

This is a take on the iconic warm turkey sandwich dressed with Mornay sauce from the famous Brown Hotel in downtown Louisville, Kentucky! Nothing says Kentucky Derby Day more than the hot brown . . . except maybe the mint julep!

MAKES 24

MORNAY SAUCE
1½ cups milk
1 small shallot, peeled
¼ teaspoon dry mustard
1 garlic clove, smashed
1 fresh thyme sprig
1 bay leaf
2 tablespoons unsalted butter
2 tablespoons all-purpose flour
Kosher salt
White pepper
Pinch ground nutmeg
⅛ teaspoon cayenne pepper
1½ cups shredded Gruyère cheese

SANDWICH
24 slices party rye or pumpernickel bread
¾ pound thinly sliced deli turkey
3 plum tomatoes, cut into 8 slices each
6 slices crispy cooked bacon, crumbled, for garnish
Freshly chopped parsley, for garnish

To make the sauce, pour the milk in a saucepan and add the shallot, mustard, garlic, thyme, and bay leaf. Warm over medium-low heat until the milk starts to steam, about 10 minutes. Remove from the heat and allow the flavors to fuse.

In a large skillet or saucepan over medium heat, melt the butter, then add the flour. Cook, whisking, for 3 to 4 minutes. Do not let brown. Strain the solids from the milk mixture, and then whisk the milk vigorously into

the roux to avoid lumps. Continue to cook, whisking constantly, until thickened, about 5 minutes. Remove from the heat and season with the salt, white pepper, nutmeg, and cayenne. Add the cheese and stir until it is melted.

Preheat the oven to broil.

To make the sandwiches, place the bread slices on a baking sheet lined with parchment paper. Top each bread slice with 1 or 2 slices of turkey, folded to fit on top of the bread. Follow with a tomato slice and 1 heaping tablespoon of sauce. Broil for 2 to 3 minutes until golden brown on top. Remove from oven and sprinkle with bacon and parsley.

MINI PULLED-PORK EGG ROLLS WITH PEACH BBQ SAUCE

These amazing egg rolls are full of three things we Southerners love: pulled pork, coleslaw, and peach barbecue sauce. Make lots . . . these will go fast!

MAKES 15 TO 20 MINI ROLLS OR 10 FULL-SIZE ROLLS

1 cup shredded white cabbage

⅓ cup shredded red cabbage

1 carrot, shredded

¼ cup mayonnaise

2 tablespoons olive oil

1 tablespoon apple cider vinegar

1 pound pulled pork

20 wonton wrappers or 10 regular egg roll wrappers

Cooking oil, for frying

Dipping sauce of choice

In a medium bowl, combine the white and red cabbages, carrot, mayonnaise, olive oil, and apple cider vinegar to create the coleslaw.

Lay out 1 wonton wrapper with one of the corners pointing toward you. Place ½ tablespoon of pulled pork and ½ tablespoon of coleslaw in the center of the wrapper (if using an egg roll wrapper, place 1 tablespoon of each filling in the wrapper). Using your fingers, wet all the edges with water. This will help the roll stay together after you roll it. Then, take the corner that's pointing toward you, and fold it up over the mixture of pulled pork and coleslaw, fold the left and right ends in, and roll it up. Repeat using the remaining ingredients.

Heat the cooking oil in a deep fryer or heavy skillet to 350 degrees F and fry the rolls for approximately 2 minutes or until golden brown. Drain on a paper towel–lined platter. Arrange on serving dish with a small bowl of sauce.

SPICY MARINATED OLIVES

A great pop-up appetizer, these herb and garlic olives are super easy to make.

MAKES APPROXIMATELY 2 CUPS

2 cups Castelvetrano or manzanilla olives
½ tablespoon dried thyme
½ tablespoon dried rosemary
½ tablespoon dried oregano
¼ teaspoon crushed red pepper flakes
2 garlic cloves, minced
¼ cup olive oil
1 teaspoon lemon zest

Mix all the ingredients in a bowl. Place in a container and refrigerate. When ready to serve, remove from refrigerator, and allow to sit for 15 minutes.

You can do this several days in advance of your event—the longer the olives marinate, the better. These will last several months in the refrigerator in an airtight container.

SPICED ALMONDS

A great, healthy appetizer for snacking or serving with wine or cocktails. Make lots—these go fast!! Use this recipe with walnuts, pecans, hazelnuts, or plain peanuts.

MAKES APPROXIMATELY 1 CUP

1 cup natural almonds
1 teaspoon olive oil
1½ teaspoons Chef Belinda Mediterranean Steak Spice
    or Cajun spice, divided
1 tablespoon honey

Preheat the oven to 325 degrees F.

Line a small baking sheet or skillet with parchment paper. In a medium bowl, toss the nuts with olive oil, 1 teaspoon of the spice, and the honey.

Spread the nuts in a single layer on the baking sheet. Roast for 20 to 25 minutes. Once out of the oven, sprinkle the remaining ½ teaspoon of spice on top of the warm nuts; mix gently to make sure all nuts are covered with the extra spice and spread out again on the baking sheet. Wait until they cool down before eating so they do not burn your mouth.

Store in a clean, lidded container. Will last up to a month. No need to refrigerate.

Acknowledgments

Katharine Brasserie + Bar in the Kimpton Cardinal Hotel in Winston-Salem, North Carolina. It has been my pleasure to live here for the past four years and bear witness to the wonderful bar and restaurant culture and atmosphere that you have created and nurtured and continue to improve upon.

Justin Rankin, bartender extraordinaire and dear friend! I have learned so much from you about spirits, cocktail-making techniques, and general bar knowledge. It is my pleasure to feature you and your cocktail in my book. I appreciate your time and your generous spirit, and I wish you the best, wherever your career takes you. I am a huge fan!

Photo credit: Justin Rankin

Martha Hopkins, my longtime agent. Thank you for doing what you do! Without you I would not be doing what I do!

Michelle Branson and all my friends at Gibbs Smith. I could do this over and over again for you . . . because you ask.

All my friends, family, and neighbors who offered themselves up for taste-testing the recipes in this book. Thanks, but I always had this!

For every bartender I ever met who was gracious enough to indulge my curiosity and to offer up your recipes, ideas, and suggestions for my book. I will always admire and see the value in what you do.

Index

Absinthe-Minded
  Martini, 42
Alligator Fart, 91
Aperol Bellini, 36
Aperol Rosé Spritz, 86
appetizers
  Apple Butter and
    Brie Tartlets, 133
  Caviar Deviled
    Quail Eggs, 127
  Crab and Artichoke
    Dip, 132
  Crab Hush
    Puppies, 125
  Homemade Pita
    Chips, 133
  Mac and Cheese
    Poppers, 126
  Mini Hot Browns,
    134–135
  Mini Pulled-Pork Egg
    Rolls with Peach
    BBQ Sauce, 136
  Mini Shrimp Cakes, 129
  Pimento Cheese and
    Tomato Sliders, 130
  Sausage Roll
    Poppers, 128
  Spiced Almonds, 138
  Spicy Marinated
    Olives, 137
Apple Butter and
  Brie Tartlets, 133
Aviation, 56

bartending golden
  rules, 11–12
beer
  Black and Tan, 101
  Black Velvet, 78
  Campari Shandy, 95
  Chelada Beer
    Cocktail, 97
  Classic Shandy, 94
  Ginger Shandy, 94
  Paloma Beer
    Cocktail, 98
  Panaché (French
    Shandy), 102
  South-of-the-Border
    Shandy, 97

Bee's Knees, 122
Berry and Peach
  Sangria, 53
Berry Fizz, 108
Berry Slush, 83
Bishop, 82
Black and Tan, 101
Black Velvet, 78
Blood Orange Texas
  Margarita, 51
Bloody Mary, Loaded, 39
bourbon
  Bourbon and Honey-
    Spice Cocktail, 25
  Bourbon Smash, 89
  Brandy Milk Punch, 121
  The Cheer Maker, 122
  Fart Heard Around
    the World, 90
  Mississippi Bourbon
    Punch, 114–115
  Mississippi Eggnog, 22
  Raspberry and
    Tarragon Smash, 88
  Southern Belle
    Martini, 70
  Southern
    Gentleman, 113
  Wine Sour, 81
brandy
  Brandy Milk Punch, 121
  Mulled Wine, 30
Bushwacker, 116

Campari
  Campari Bicycle
    Cocktail, 78
  Campari Shandy, 95
  Classic Campari
    Spritz, 86
  Negroni, 45
Cardamom, Cinnamon,
  and Star Anise–
  Infused Vodka, 19
Cardinal, 81
Caviar Deviled
  Quail Eggs, 127
champagne
  Black Velvet, 78
  Champagne
    Cocktail, 33

Chef B's Citrus-
  Champagne
  Sangria, 59
Kir Royale, 77
Megmosa, 40
Merry Cranberry
  Mimosa, 24
New Orleans Citrus-
  Pomegranate
  Punch, 34
Soixante-Quinze
  (French75), 21
The Cheer Maker, 122
Chef B's Citrus-
  Champagne Sangria, 59
Chelada Beer Cocktail, 97
Cherry-Lime Rickey, 104
Chili-Infused Vodka, 19
Chocolate Martini, 67
Cider Sidecar, 33
Classic Campari
  Spritz, 86
Classic Martini, 66
Classic Shandy, 94
cocktails, about, 9–14
Coconut Mojito, 55
cognac
  Chef B's Citrus-
    Champagne
    Sangria, 59
  Cider Sidecar, 33
  Soixante-Quinze
    (French75), 21
  Vieux Carré, 117
Crab and Artichoke
  Dip, 132
Crab Hush Puppies, 125

Dirty Cajun Martini, 69
Duck Fart, 90

Eggnog, Mississippi, 22
equipment, 12–13
Espresso Martini, 73

farts, 85
  Alligator Fart, 91
  Duck Fart, 90
  Fart Heard Around
    the World, 90
  Monkey Fart, 91

French 75 (Soixante-Quinze), 21

gin
Absinthe-Minded Martini, 42
Aviation, 56
Bee's Knees, 122
Classic Martini, 66
Negroni, 45
Pimm's Cup, 119
Tennessee Iced Tea, 46
Ginger Shandy, 94
Ginger-Honey Lemonade, 110

Homemade Pita Chips, 133
Hot Buttered Rum, 26

In-the-Woods Moon-shine Cocktail, 63
Irish Coffee, 29
Irish cream
Bushwacker, 116
Chocolate Martini, 67
Duck Fart, 90
Peppermint Martini, 74

Jägermeister
Alligator Fart, 91

Kahlúa
Bushwacker, 116
Duck Fart, 90
Kir Royale, 77

Lavender Simple Syrup, 17
layering, 14
Lemon Drop Martini, 66
lemonade
Ginger-Honey Lemonade, 110
Moonshine Lemonade, 60
Pimm's Cup, 119
Sparkling Blueberry Lemonade, 107
Sparkling Vodka Lemonade, 40
Vodka Strawberry Lemonade, 62
Lillet Burnt-Orange Twist, 36
Lilletini, 72
Loaded Bloody Mary, 39

Mac and Cheese Poppers, 126
Mango Colada, 54
Margarita, Blood Orange Texas, 51
Martinis, 64–65
Absinthe-Minded Martini, 42
Chocolate Martini, 67
Classic Martini, 66
Dirty Cajun Martini, 69
Espresso Martini, 73
Lemon Drop Martini, 66
Lilletini, 72
Peppermint Martini, 74
Pickletini, 70
Pineapple Martini, 69
Southern Belle Martini, 70
Megmosa, 40
Merry Cranberry Mimosa, 24
Mimosa, Merry Cranberry, 24
Mini Hot Browns, 134–135
Mini Pulled-Pork Egg Rolls with Peach BBQ Sauce, 136
Mini Shrimp Cakes, 129
Mint Simple Syrup, 17
Mississippi Bourbon Punch, 114–115
Mississippi Eggnog, 22
mocktails
Berry Fizz, 108
Cherry-Lime Rickey, 104
Ginger-Honey Lemonade, 110
Pineapple Citrus Tropical, 107
Pineapple Ginger Beer, 109
Pomegranate Paloma, 104
Sparkling Blueberry Lemonade, 107
Watermelon Spritz, 110
Mojito, Coconut, 55
Monkey Fart, 91
Moonshine Lemonade, 60
muddling, 14
Mulled Wine, 30

Negroni, 45
New Orleans Citrus-Pomegranate Punch, 34

Orange Crush, 48

Paloma, 45
Paloma Beer Cocktail, 98
Panaché (French Shandy), 102
Peppermint Martini, 74
Pickletini, 70
Pimento Cheese and Tomato Sliders, 130
Pimm's Cup, 119
Pineapple Citrus Tropical, 107
Pineapple Ginger Beer, 109
Pineapple Martini, 69
Plain Simple Syrup, 16
Pomegranate Paloma, 104
prosecco
Aperol Bellini, 36
Classic Campari Spritz, 86
Southern Gentleman, 113

Raspberry and Tarragon Smash, 88
Rosemary Simple Syrup, 16
Rosemary-Infused Vodka, 18
rum
Bishop, 82
Bushwacker, 116
Coconut Mojito, 55
Hot Buttered Rum, 26
Mango Colada, 54
Mississippi Eggnog, 22
Rum Runner, 115
Tennessee Iced Tea, 46

sangrias
Berry and Peach Sangria, 53
Chef B's Citrus-Champagne Sangria, 59
Tequila Sangria, 77
Sausage Roll Poppers, 128
1792 Kentucky White Dog Julep, 60
shaking, 14
shandies
Campari Shandy, 95
Classic Shandy, 94

Ginger Shandy, 94
Panaché (French
    Shandy), 102
South-of-the-Border
    Shandy, 97
smashes, 85
    Bourbon Smash, 89
    Raspberry and
        Tarragon Smash, 88
Soixante-Quinze
    (French75), 21
Southern Belle Martini, 70
Southern Gentleman, 113
Southern Mule, 101
South-of-the-Border
    Shandy, 97
Sparkling Blueberry
    Lemonade, 107
Sparkling Vodka
    Lemonade, 40
Spiced Almonds, 138
Spiced-Honey Syrup, 18
Spicy Marinated
    Olives, 137
spritzes, 84–85
    Aperol Rosé Spritz, 86
    Classic Campari
        Spritz, 86
    Watermelon Spritz, 110
stirring, 14
Swamp Water, 49
Sweet Tea Mule, 120
syrups
    Lavender Simple
        Syrup, 17
    Mint Simple Syrup, 17
    Plain Simple Syrup, 16
    Rosemary Simple
        Syrup, 16

Spiced-Honey
    Syrup, 18

techniques, 13–14
Tennessee Iced Tea, 46
tequila, 46
    Blood Orange Texas
        Margarita, 51
    Monkey Fart, 91
    Paloma, 45
    Paloma Beer
        Cocktail, 98
    Tequila Sangria, 77
    Texas Ranch Water, 119
Texas Ranch Water, 119

Vieux Carré, 117
vodka
    Cardamom, Cinnamon,
        and Star Anise–
        Infused Vodka, 19
    Chili-Infused Vodka, 19
    Chocolate Martini, 67
    Classic Martini, 66
    Dirty Cajun Martini, 69
    Espresso Martini, 73
    Lemon Drop Martini, 66
    Lilletini, 72
    Loaded Bloody
        Mary, 39
    Orange Crush, 48
    Peppermint Martini, 74
    Pickletini, 70
    Pineapple Martini, 69
    Rosemary-Infused
        Vodka, 18
    Southern Mule, 101
    Sparkling Vodka
        Lemonade, 40

Sweet Tea Mule, 120
Tennessee Iced Tea, 46
Vodka Strawberry
    Lemonade, 62

Watermelon Spritz, 110
whiskey
    Duck Fart, 90
    Irish Coffee, 29
    Moonshine
        Lemonade, 60
    1792 Kentucky White
        Dog Julep, 60
    Tennessee Iced Tea, 46
    Vieux Carré, 117
    In-the-Woods
        Moonshine
        Cocktail, 63
wine. See also
    Champagne; prosecco
    Aperol Rosé Spritz, 86
    Berry and Peach
        Sangria, 53
    Berry Slush, 83
    Bishop, 82
    Campari Bicycle
        Cocktail, 78
    Cardinal, 81
    Chef B's Citrus-
        Champagne
        Sangria, 59
    Mississippi Bourbon
        Punch, 114–115
    Mulled Wine, 30
    New Orleans Citrus-
        Pomegranate
        Punch, 34
    Tequila Sangria, 77
    Wine Sour, 81

METRIC CONVERSION CHART

Volume Measurements		Weight Measurements		Temperature Conversion	
U.S.	METRIC	U.S.	METRIC	FAHRENHEIT	CELSIUS
1 teaspoon	5 ml	½ ounce	15 g	250	120
1 tablespoon	15 ml	1 ounce	30 g	300	150
¼ cup	60 ml	3 ounces	90 g	325	160
⅓ cup	75 ml	4 ounces	115 g	350	180
½ cup	125 ml	8 ounces	225 g	375	190
⅔ cup	150 ml	12 ounces	350 g	400	200
¾ cup	175 ml	1 pound	450 g	425	220
1 cup	250 ml	2¼ pounds	1 kg	450	230

About the Author

Belinda Smith-Sullivan is a chef, food writer, spice blends entrepreneur, and commercially rated pilot. She has a culinary arts degree from Johnson & Wales University, and is a monthly food columnist for *South Carolina Living Magazine.* She also is featured on *South Carolina Living*'s website with monthly how-to videos. Smith-Sullivan is an active member of the Southern Foodways Alliance, International Association of Culinary Professionals, and the International Food Wine and Travel Writers Association, American Culinary Federation, and Les Dames d'Escoffier. She lives in Winston-Salem, North Carolina.

Author photo taken at The Katharine Brasserie + Bar, Winston-Salem, North Carolina, by photographer Sharlie Brown